PUTTING POWER IN ITS PLACE:

Create Community Control!

Edited by
Christopher Plant & Judith Plant

The New Catalyst Bioregional Series

NEW SOCIETY PUBLISHERS
Philadelphia, PA   Gabriola Island, BC

Canadian Cataloguing in Publication Data

Main entry under title:
Putting Power In Its Place

(The New Catalyst Bioregional Series; 3)
Includes bibliographical references.
ISBN 1-55092-158-4 (bound); -- ISBN 1-55092-159-2 (pbk.)

1. Community power. 2. Community organization. 3. Decentralization in government.
I. Plant, Christopher M.   II. Plant, Judith.   III. Series.
HN49.P6P88 1991   303.3   C91-091413-3

Inquiries regarding requests to reprint all or part of *Putting Power In Its Place* should be
addressed to:
New Society Publishers,
4527 Springfield Avenue, Philadelphia PA, USA 19143,
or
P.O. Box 189, Gabriola Island B.C., Canada V0R 1X0.

USA: ISBN 0-86571-216-6 Hardback
USA: ISBN 0-86571-217-4 Paperback
Canada: ISBN 1-55092-158-4 Hardback
Canada: ISBN 1-55092-159-2 Paperback

Cover design by George Gaia.

Book design and typesetting by *The New Catalyst/New Society Publishers*, Canada.

Printed in the United States of America on partially recycled paper by
Capital City Press, Montpelier, Vermont.

To order directly from the publishers, please add $2.50 to the price for the first copy,
75 cents each additional. Send check or money order to:
New Society Publishers
4527 Springfield Avenue, Philadelphia PA, USA 19143
or
P.O. Box 189, Gabriola Island B.C., Canada V0R 1X0.

New Society Publishers is a project of the New Society Educational Foundation, a non-
profit, tax-exempt public foundation in the U.S. and the Catalyst Education Society, a
non-profit educational society in Canada. Opinions expressed in this book do not
necessarily represent positions of the New Society Educational Foundation, nor the
Catalyst Education Society.

Putting Power In Its Place is the third of *The New Catalyst*'s Bioregional Series. The
Bioregional Series is available by subscription, subscribers also receiving *The New
Catalyst Quarterly* free of charge. Write: P.O. Box 189, Gabriola Island B.C.,
Canada V0R 1X0.

The New Catalyst Bioregional Series

The New Catalyst magazine was published for five years from the dry interior of British Columbia, some 20 miles along a gravel road from the nearest town. In this rural setting of Douglas fir and Ponderosa pine just west of the coast mountain range, a small community has been slowly building over the past decade or so, dedicated to trying to live an alternative to the Megamachine which threatens to destroy life on this planet. Part of this experiment has been *The New Catalyst*, published regularly by a tiny editorial collective since the fall of 1985, the product of home-generated electric power from a creek, as well as of much love and volunteer labor.

From the beginning, an important aim of *The New Catalyst* was to act as a catalyst among the diverse strands of the alternative movement—to break through the overly sharp dividing lines between environmentalists and aboriginal nations; peace activists and permaculturalists; feminists, food co-ops, city-reinhabitants and back-to-the-landers—to promote healthy dialogue among all these tendencies working for progressive change, for a new world. Early on, it became clear that the emerging bioregional movement was itself something of a catalyst and umbrella for these groups, too. Subsequently, but without announcing the fact, *The New Catalyst* became a bioregional journal for the north west, consciously attempting to draw together the local efforts of people engaged in both resistance and renewal from as far apart as northern British Columbia, Alberta and California, as well as the broader, more global thinking of key people from elsewhere in North America and around the world.

Seeking to inspire the courageous struggle to forge alternatives among communities near and far, the magazine reached an appreciative, but limited, readership. To broaden this readership—a task we deem urgent in this "turn-around" decade—in the spring of 1990, *The New Catalyst* made an experimental move to Gabriola Island, one of the Gulf Islands in British Columbia's Strait of Georgia. With a change of format, *The New Catalyst* is now reorganized to primarily include material of regional importance, and is distributed free in many more thousands of copies than we could have published previously. At the same time, material of relevance to a wider audience—to all Turtle Island and beyond—is now published twice yearly in *The New Catalyst*'s Bioregional Series of books.

The Bioregional Series builds upon the wealth of experience gained from people actually living and creating alternatives to global monoculture in their many diverse ways. It aims to inspire and stimulate the building of new, ecologically sustainable cultures in their myriad facets through presenting a broad spectrum of concerns ranging from how we view the world and act within it, through efforts at restoring damaged ecosystems or greening the cities, to the raising of a new and hopeful generation. The Bioregional Series is designed not for those content with merely saving what's left, but for those forward- looking folk with abundant energy for life, upon whom the future of Earth depends.

The New Catalyst magazine and the *Bioregional Series* are available at a substantial discount by subscription. Write for details to: *The New Catalyst*, P.O. Box 189, Gabriola Island, B.C., Canada V0R 1X0.

Table of Contents

1. Brush Fires, Or The Bioregional Vision? An Introduction
   Christopher & Judith Plant 1

Part 1: Power Out Of Place: The Context 9

2. Local Power Versus Global Profits: The Odds Against
   Frank Tester 10

Part 2: Small Ideas: Conceiving Of Community
   Control 19

3. "Free And Equal Intercourse:" The Decentralist Design
   Kirkpatrick Sale 20
4. The Best Government Comes In Small Packages
   John Papworth 28
5. Dis-Union Now!
   Leopold Kohr 32
6. From Roadblocks To Building Blocks: Developing A
   Theory For Putting Power In Its Place
   Don Alexander 38
   * Reclaiming The Power Of Community
     Priscilla Boucher 47
7. Our Home And Native Land? Creating
   An Eco-Constitution in Canada
   Michael M'Gonigle 49
8. The Meaning Of Confederalism
   Murray Bookchin 59
   * Draft Of A Constitutional Declaration of Local
     Sovereignty
     Tom Reveille 67

**Part 3: Power In Place: Community Control
In Action** 69

9. **Land Of The Free, Home Of The Brave:
Iroquois Democracy**
Oren Lyons 70
10. **Bringing Power Back Home: A Blueprint From Vermont**
Frank Bryan &John McClaughry 76
* Seven Decentralist Strategies
Carol Moore 81
11. **Shadow Government**
George Tukel 84
12. **Watershed Stewardship: The Village Of Hazelton
Experience**
Alice Maitland & Doug Aberley 91
13. **Community Forest Boards: Gaining Control
Of Our Forests**
Herb Hammond 100
14. **The Temagami Stewardship Council**
Mary Laronde with Judith Harris 104
15. **The Need For Local Currencies**
Robert Swann 110
16. **A Metamorphosis For Cities: From Gray To Green**
Peter Berg 118
* Workers, Communities And Toxics
Eric Mann 127
17. **Two Kinds Of Power: A Different Experience At Oka**
Helen Forsey 129

Acknowledgments

Grateful acknowledgment is made for permission to reprint previously published articles from the following sources:

"Local Power Versus Global Profits," by Frank Tester was first published as a presentation entitled "Transnational Corporate Interests in British Columbia: Environmental & Social Implications," for the Save Georgia Strait Conference, 1991 (Box 122, Gabriola Island BC V0R 1X0), and is extracted and reprinted with permission.

"The Best Government Comes in Small Packages," by John Papworth was first published in *The Fourth World Review* (24 Abercorn Place, London NW8, U.K.) and *The Ecologist* Nov./Dec.1988 (M.I.T. Press Journals, 55 Hayward St., Cambridge MA 02142), and is reprinted with permission.

"Dis-Union Now!" by Leopold Kohr was first published in *The Commonweal* in 1941 and is reprinted with permission of the author.

"The Meaning of Confederalism," by Murray Bookchin was first published in *Green Perspectives*, No.20 (© 1990; P.O. Box 111, Burlington VT 05402) and is reprinted with permission of the author.

"Land Of The Free, Home Of The Brave: Iroquois Democracy," by Oren Lyons was first published in *Indian Roots of American Democracy, Northeast Indian Quarterly*, Vol.IV No.4 & Vol.5 No.1 (American Indian Program, Cornell University, Ithaca NY 14853) and is reprinted with permission.

"Bringing Power Back Home: A Blueprint From Vermont," by Frank Bryan and John McClaughry is excerpted and reprinted with permission from *The Vermont Papers: Recreating Democracy on a Human Scale* (Chelsea Green, 1989).

"Seven Decentralist Strategies," by Carol Moore is reprinted with permission of the author.

"Shadow Government," by George Tukel is excerpted and reprinted with permission from *Shadow Government* (Reinhabit The Hudson Estuary, 1986).

"Community Forest Boards: Gaining Control Of Our Forests," by Herb Hammond was first published in *Forest Planning Canada*, Vol.6, No.6 (P.O. Box 6234, Stn.C, Victoria BC V8P 5L5) and is reprinted with permission.

"The Temagami Stewardship Council," by Judith Harris was first published in *Alternatives*, Vol.17, No. 4 (c/- Faculty of Environmental Studies, University of Waterloo, Waterloo ON N2L 3G1) and is reprinted with permission.

"The Need For Local Currencies," by Bob Swann was first published as a pamphlet for the E.F. Schumacher Society (Box 76, RD 3, Great Barrington MA 01230) and is reprinted with permission.

"A Metamorphosis For Cities: From Gray To Green," by Peter Berg was first published in *City Lights Review* No.4 (San Fransisco) and is reprinted with permission.

"Workers, Communities And Toxics," by Eric Mann is extracted from "Environmentalism In The Corporate Climate," first published in *Tikkun* Vol.5, No.2, and reprinted with permission of the author and Labor/Community WATCHDOG, a social justice, worker's rights and environmental organisation in Los Angeles (14540 Haynes St., Suite 200, Van Nuys CA 91411).

1

Brush Fires
Or The Bioregional Vision?
An Introduction

Christopher & Judith Plant

S aving the world by saving the watersheds...? It's hard to describe succinctly what bioregionalism is all about to someone who has never heard the term, and from time to time we've found such turns of phrase to be useful in conveying the full sweep of the bioregional strategy. But like the expression "think globally, act locally," they are over-simplified statements of how to act in a complex world.

The bioregionalist goal is nothing short of global change. And while this might seem to be a paradox for a regionally-based strategy, it incorporates the idea that everything is connected, that without people everywhere taking responsibility for their home-places, no-one can count on a healthy and sustainable world community. This reflects an understanding of the spiritual message of land-based peoples: that the land is sacred and that the quality of all our relationships—with each other and with the natural world—determines the kind of people we are. In an ideal world, eco-communities would be spiritually and constitutionally bound by an ethic of love and respect for all of life that went beyond our own watersheds to encompass the wider world.

However, the political and economic reality of the day works against such a bioregional vision. What we are up against is a complex, co-optive, and destructive world system, with its parts knotted tightly together; and we rarely see an easy way of untangling the mess. The key question, then, is how to put the power of decision-making in the hands of those who will bear the consequences, *and* how to keep it there.

A Story Of "Right" Versus "Might"

One of the most powerful events that we've ever experienced happened in the little town of Ashcroft, in the interior of British Columbia. In summer this place is hot and dusty, but the people who live there are not transients and they know how to handle the heat—unlike the corporate executives of the transnational waste management company and their government partners, who sweated buckets that night in the town hall.

The townspeople had gathered to hear the final sales pitch for a toxic waste incinerator slated for construction on the outskirts of their town. According to popular rumor, the people had never before shown up in such numbers. It was participatory democracy in action as speaker after speaker got up to the microphone and told these polished PR professionals that they could pack up their flip charts and glossy brochures and go back to their corporate towers, or wherever it was they came from. It was not that this little town couldn't have used a few more jobs; rather, that these people love their place, value their clean water above all else and would not sell their children's futures to anyone. They'd done their homework and were not about to be confused again by these authoritative executives.

This town meeting didn't just happen. Ordinary folks, who had earlier suspected the public relations displays in the mall and the fancy cars driving elected officials around the region, had dug into the history of this company and found after-the-fact disasters and communities elsewhere who were suffering as a result. Files of information were gathered and the night the out-of-towners got the message loud and clear, all the muck was presented and all the right questions asked—it was a wonderful display of right versus might.

What remains in the minds of the people who were there that night is the heady power of the people. A threatened community stood up for itself with higher values than profit; the experience sparked a flush of pride at taking collective responsibility. Some felt that democracy was alive and well, that all you had to do was get organized and stand by the truth. Two thoughts, however, modify that initial spark of success.

First, despite Ashcroft's victory, almost everyone knew that the company would simply go down the road with their scheme until they found a community that would allow their enterprise. And, sure enough, it did. Of course, it was pre-empted as much as possible. Those files of information were quickly copied and forwarded on down the line. But that, ultimately, isn't enough. Not-In-My-Back-Yard (NIMBY) struggles can indeed succeed, but rarely do they change the overall status quo. The structural factors that made such an invasion possible all remain.

Second, it was evident that this community's success was based on the overwhelming unity of the townspeople. More often than not, a town would be more divided in its response, with some locals having vested interests in the "outsider" scheme. Clearly in such a case, even if power were held locally, the outcome could be very different. Local power is not always benign.

These folks were lucky, and they knew it. Everyone knows, and some from direct experience, that if that company and government had been really intent on getting their way, they have plenty of might, of power-over, with which to "persuade"—from high-powered public relations schemes and economic squeezes, to police forces and even the army—as the Mohawks of Oka, for example, know only too well. (See Helen Forsey's moving account of the Oka crisis in Part Three.)

So, while these back yard struggles might sometimes be successful and it will look like democracy is working, in the final analysis, the very structure of our so-called democratic system will not have changed one bit. If the people are not continually vigilant, they may lose the next time around. In fact, nearby the town of Ashcroft, barely a few months later, a massive landfill site was built in order to bury Vancouver's garbage to be trucked from 200 miles away...

What We're Up Against: Power-Out-Of-Place

Stories like the one from Ashcroft crop up regularly in the alternative press. For example, in India, too, the forests have long been under attack, prompting an ingenious demonstration: the "Pluck and Plant" protest. Here the people refused to have their commonly-held forest lands turned into eucalyptus plantations for the Birlas—one of the richest corporations in the country. Instead, the "industrial" eucalyptus trees were plucked from the ground and replaced with trees that could be of use to the community.

Sometimes successful, oftentimes not, these communities are confronting the same power: that held by distant corporations who have manipulated governments through promises of jobs and other economic gains to take away the land. If governments are paving the way for these corporate giants, who will take the part of local communities? And who will stand up for all the other species on this planet: the birds, the trees, the animals, and the rest of the non-human world? With high finance, global mass markets, and corporate gain as the fundamental starting point, a community's development becomes a game of Russian roulette for local people and places. Decision-making power, in spite of democracy so-called, is out-of-place. Subsequently, the tenacious struggle for humankind's essential "right"—to assume responsibility for the well-being of the places called home—emerges over and over again.

In our experience here in the northwest—a significant resource basket for the industrial centers of the world—the features of these local "brush fires" possess a characteristic pattern. Usually the confrontation in question, whether over forests or fisheries, wilderness or free-flowing rivers, leads to acute polarization of the community. Just as wilderness is valued against jobs (as though having both is not also an option), workers are pitted against "environmentalists" and "single interest groups," or against native peoples. When, all along, the companies are calling the shots, and the governments are smoothing their way. Frequently, the polarization is intentional and manufactured. And the aim is always the same: to remove the people (or render them powerless at least) and take (or use up) the land. The technical term used by land use planners and others for this act is revealing: it is to *alienate* the land, and the people—to make alien, disconnected, "other." It's a bit like putting out brush fires all over the planet and never quite being able to deal with the pyromaniac. Power-out-of-place, having roots in no place nor allegiance to any people, is the *modus operandi* of today's political and economic machine, the latest variant of which is dubbed the "New World Order." From an ecological perspective, growth without limits (what the New World Order will defend to the death) could be likened to a cancer that will cease only when its host dies.

This tragedy stems from a huge blind spot: the inability of power out-of-place to take into account that life is sacred, that what it so successfully alienates and uses for its own self-interest is part of the life-blood of all living things. It is corporate empire: self-interested, greedy, and fearful of anything that is different, and it asserts its muscle relentlessly against those who dare question its authority. Deeply cynical, it is power as control. Its hallmark is alienation, and its consequence the destruction of the Earth.

People And Place Unite: The Tin Wis Coalition

This book was inspired by a particular event that we attended last fall which seemed to go one step further than most "brush fire" struggles. It was the second of what is shaping up to be a process rather than an event, and was set in the context of nation-wide strife over resource issues that has often left workers, environmentalists and native people fighting among themselves. It gathered these separate groups together under one roof with the specific aim of identifying common foes and common interests.

George Watts, a spokesperson for the Nuu-Chah-Nulth Indian people on whose land we were meeting, explained in his welcome to everyone, why, for him, this event was different. He said that, unlike many of the newcomers to his territory, his security would never be found in his job; that he would never dream of leaving his *real* security—his family, his people and his place—for higher wages somewhere else; and he was hoping that others were having the same idea.

The diverse mix of keen participants was really heartening, for what this gathering was attempting to do was find common ground, in spite of differences, and organize from that basis. Amongst the crowd were Nuu-Chah-Nulth leaders and spokespeople, local and regional labor people from the IWA (International Woodworkers of America) and Fisherman's Union, grassroots environmentalists, far-sighted academics, elected and non-elected political party people, and ordinary, non-aligned citizens. All had in common a concern for the vast power held over the citizenry in their communities by the mega-corporations and their government hand-maidens. All felt that in some way or another they were being dealt a raw deal. All were trying to grapple with the fact that unless we could get along and work together, we were going to remain divided and eventually, one by one, be conquered.

Over the few days that we were together, sitting around conference tables looking our differences squarely in the face, it became apparent that we were asking ourselves to do more than just elect the right politicians. This business of working together meant overcoming our own fears, it meant letting go enough of each of our own, often tightly held, points of view, so that we might all work together. This meant, for non-native people, for instance, that we had to get firmly behind native land claims which, in turn, ultimately meant dealing with our own racism. And native people were being asked, once again, to trust white people, in spite of years of abuse. Politicians were being asked to be accountable to the local people, no matter what their party lines, and to realise that centralized policies frequently don't make sense. Environmentalists were being asked to go beyond preservationism, to see the land as something we need to learn to use with sensitivity, not abuse, nor keep like a ship in a bottle.

On a deep level, we were exploring whether or not we could trust each other. Could we open up our hearts and minds and find some way to allow each other our "piece of the truth," to reach consensus, or were the differences simply too enormous? At some point, many realized that what we were asking of ourselves was whether we cared enough about the places and people we love to transcend the fear of difference and its hierarchical solutions—the personal baggage inherited from western culture—so that we all might move beyond self-righteousness and self-interest? After all, in nature diversity is the sign of a healthy and stable ecosystem. Without embracing our own diversity, the various organizations and factions would continue to be limited to single issue struggles. But by building common ground, this coalition could do more than fight corporate forestry practices, for example. Rooted in the familiar territory of place, it could begin to create a community where our differences could work together for the common well-being of both people and place.

Communities Taking Control

While brush fires continue to crop up everywhere, this more thoughtful, over-arching and sustained kind of work found in the Tin Wis example is increasingly engaging people's attention. Bioregional congresses, both regionally and continent-wide, have been drawing together truly diverse mixes of people: back-to-the-landers rubbing shoulders with feminists and native peoples, home-spun ecologists swapping information with Town Planners, Christian clerics discussing spirituality with pagans and witches, permaculturalists and forest activists learning from the new "urban pioneers".... Alliances and coalitions are the order of the day.

From our experience in our own bioregion—the Gulf Islands of B.C.'s west coast—a powerful gathering of a wide range of interest groups, from local activists and labor unions to political parties and island governments, recently formed the Save Georgia Strait Alliance to give stronger focus to the work that each is doing locally, as well as greater clout at the level of the bioregion as a whole. And to counter the ease with which we local folk are divided, coalitions like the Tin Wis of previously distinct and polarized groups are forming, their intent to expressly find the common ground on which they can be united.

From the stories in this book and from other examples far and wide, we see the promise of the fact that these tendencies reflect the long and often painful learning experienced over many years of battling centralized authorities. There'a new willingness to listen, a new tolerance of others and respect for where they're coming from. They indicate, too, a certain sophistication born of trial and error, and an understanding of both the nature of power, and the real work ahead. The bioregional congresses, for example, are seen by their participants as shadow governments run by and for the people (and other species) of a region. As the credibility of the central governments now in power declines, the idea is that these congresses will gradually replace the tired old forms or, at least, be places where new, appropriate forms of governance can be engendered.

At the root of these initiatives is the strongly-held desire to change the kind of power at work, in a multitude of dimensions:

• First, the locus of real authority is everywhere being challenged. Distant centers of power, dominated by their bureaucrats and bankers, are seen by more and more people to have had their day. Instead there is a strident call for local control of local affairs. There is confidence emerging in the power of people in place, people protecting their homes, acting for the long-term, by *self*-government. The loss of local power is perceived increasingly to be undermining the very ability of local people to survive over time in a sustainable way. In place of the fear, division and distrust that this engenders there is, here and there, a willingness to work together despite the differences, a confidence in the ability of ordinary people. And, as an understanding of ecology permeates more and more, this call is made not just in the interests of human populations, but increasingly on behalf of the rest of the natural world, too.

• Second, rounding out this understanding, is the knowledge that local control alone is only part of the solution. Necessary, but not sufficient, the full-blown vision needs confederation of empowered local groups as a vital ingredient.

• Third, the circle is an increasingly common feature of these initiatives. Decisions are frequently made not by Robert's Rules of Order (a method designed for use by hierarchies, with the inevitable by-product of majorities and minorities, a divided whole), but by consensus, a method that values each person's part of the truth and which promotes the commonality of purpose in a group rather than the divisions it might contain.

• Fourth, there is a growing awareness that the kind of independent power that is sought goes beyond the political realm to include the economic base and culture of communities. Gaining self-government invariably means breaking the circle of dependence upon the global economy, reducing our consumption of its cheap commodities, and creating local and regional economies and cultures that genuinely sustain local life.

• Finally, thanks in large part to the growing presence and leadership of native peoples in these struggles, as well as to an increasing ability to hear the voice of feminists, there is a slow but steady realisation that western civilization, in its typical alienated way, has got the very nature of power all wrong—that there is a power beyond the power to control. A greater power, for sure, a power that comes with our responsibility as one species among many: the power to restrain our desires, to rein in our technical abilities, the power to see the whole and act with sensitivity within it. Among the Mondragon cooperatives of Spain, this power is termed the pursuit of "equilibrio." And equilibrio is seen as not just equilibrium or balance, but also harmony, poise, calmness, composure—a vital process that harmonizes and balances a growing community of interests, from the individual outward to the community and environment.

There is a widely-felt need, therefore, to transform the very nature of power, to put it back *in place*, to empower local communities and, on that basis, to confederate and create a newly powerful form: a truly ecological and sustainable whole. The fate of the Earth hangs in the balance....

Part One

Power Out Of Place: The Context

As community-minded folk, we are finding ourselves in an absurd situation: major decisions affecting local places are, almost always, made from some distant, centralized government or corporate offices. The more impact on the small region, municipality and even neighborhood, the further away seem to be the decision-makers.

Inevitably, then, decisions are made that do not take into account the knowledge that can only come from knowing a place through years, indeed generations, of inhabitation. For the interests from afar are fleeting and have to do solely with profiteering and not long-term health and sustainability—the large corporation can always go elsewhere. Thus, trying to take responsibility for the well-being of the places we call home leads grassroots organizations into complex and contradictory situations. At issue is finding a way to shift the power back home where the possibility for democratic and ecological integrity lies. And the urgency is to do so before we find ourselves to be the powerless, feudalized peasantry of the transnational corporations.

2

Local Power
Versus Global Profits:
The Odds Against

Frank Tester

The extent to which our lives are governed by global forces is becoming more apparent as ecological limits are approached. The almost universal call for more power to be devolved to the community level occurs in the context of a world where power is daily more concentrated in fewer and fewer hands. As this process of consolidation continues, the hopeful optimism of the "Global Village" idea— where new technologies promised to usher in a new era of decentralized and more equitable development for all—has given way to the frightening reality of the unfettered transnational corporation. By nature amoral, by design profitable above all other considerations, this new corporate form owes allegiance to no place on Earth. Exerting huge influence over the day-to-day management of our lives, the "new" corporations—with the help of "free market" governments— are re- feudalizing modern society to an extent never previously imagined.

Typical of this phenomenon is our own bioregion—the Gulf Islands of Canada's west coast—and the wider, resource-rich province of British Columbia in general. Frank Tester, a professor at the University of British Columbia's School of Social Work, describes the odds against the decentralist impulse in this particular part of the world—the same odds that face attempts in many other places to authentically localise the decision-making process. His analysis provides a sobering, "realistic" depiction of the problem of power we are up against, a backdrop for the more optimistic articles to follow.

Transnational corporations control an increasingly large percentage of global economic activity. In B.C., this economic activity includes the forest industry, fishing, mining and agriculture. Fletcher Challenge, for example, is a New Zealand transnational corporation (TNC)—one of the biggest forest companies in the province. Resource extraction activities dominated by TNCs are increasing their role in shaping the social and environmental conditions of the Georgia Strait region which includes the cities of Vancouver and Victoria—about 70 percent of the province's total population.

Environmental, labor and other popular movements need to better understand how TNCs and the global economy operate, and what this might mean for local, as well as global, environmental and social conditions.

The "Nature" Of Transnational Corporations

The term "transnational corporation" is not merely a synonym for "multinational corporation." Multinational corporations are companies operating *in* more than one nation. TNCs are companies operating not only *in* many countries, but *across* national borders. This is not a trivial difference. TNCs must be understood in the context of a push toward global free trade, where trade increasingly takes place in global markets unencumbered by tariff and non-tariff barriers to trade.

The presence of national boundaries is increasingly irrelevant to the activities of TNCs. In other words, control of a nation's economic affairs by national governments, consistent with the traditional goals of business, is diminished and the "logic" of the market, conceived on a global scale, determines the nature, structure and functions of national economies. Global free trade is designed to severely curtail the extent to which governments can manage national economies for social as well as economic purposes.

What many environmentalists and others working for social change fail to appreciate is the logic which is inherent in the structural arrangements of a global capitalist economy. The exigencies of corporate behaviour originate within the logic of the system *in and of itself.* If Adam Zimmerman, the president of Noranda, experienced a "conversion" tomorrow, he would simply be replaced.

TNCs benefit from the financial arrangements which global operations make possible. Transfer pricing is perhaps the most important of these. Through transfer pricing, a corporation may get around any limits or restrictions placed on profit-making in a particular country, or may price raw materials or other stages in the production process so that specific operations actually appear to lose money, while the overall corporation remains profitable. In such a case, the profit has been transferred to another corporate division, perhaps located in another jurisdiction. These devices can be used not only to avoid or reduce taxes, but to control labor and to argue against monies being spent on social, environmental and other benefits.

One of the assumptions underlying the logic of a globalized economy is that a global system which is free from humanly-made impediments to business activity will be maximally efficient in its use of human labor and materials. Global competition puts added pressure on corporations to increase the efficiency of their operations because competition is, in the absence of national boundaries, greatly increased by the presence in the market of producers from all over the world—not merely from within the country in question. This competition puts additional pressure on corporations to reduce their costs of production and/or expand their markets. This can be done in a limited number of ways: reduce wages; replace labor with technology—as in the B.C. forest industry; reduce monies spent on addressing the environmental and social costs of production; locate or relocate to wherever labor and other costs are minimal (the Maquiladora region of Mexico, for instance, where wages are US$4.00 a day on average); develop new products; create new consumer needs and meet them; capture markets from competitors. All of these measures have serious environmental and social implications.

Environmental And Social Implications

The globalization of the world economy has major negative implications for the development and enforcement of environmental standards both in B.C. and internationally. Meeting environmental standards costs money. Corporations operating in B.C. must now face competition on a global scale from TNCs based elsewhere.

It is therefore a mistake to look at the profit level in the industry and conclude that it can afford to spend money meeting environmental standards. This only makes sense if one assumes that a corporation is more or less contained within national boundaries and has a somewhat limited outlet for its capital. Corporate resistance to meeting tough new standards—even where corporations have generated phenomenal profits and given the activities taking place in a globalized economy—is understandable. In order to stay competitive and to have a presence in what is now a global market, Canadian corporate interests need as much capital as they can get for overseas investment. It is not necessarily in the interests of Macmillan Bloedel to let a Japanese forest firm acquire the rights to pulp wood in Australia and other places. In other words, the global economy has made the possibility (and necessity) of foreign investment and the modernization of productive processes in order to remain competitive, an increasingly limitless struggle.

This makes the regulatory situation all the more desperate. Evidence of this can be found in the recent outcome of attempts to establish a 1.5 kilogram organochlorines/tonne-of-pulp limit on discharges to B.C. coastal waters by 1994. The industry apparently didn't like the new rules suggested by former Environment Minister John Reynolds. It appears that he resigned when the premier, Bill Vander Zalm, caved in to industry pressure and committed the government to a limit of 2.5 kilograms/tonne. The political power of the Canadian forest industry has always been considerable and is as strong now as ever, given that forest products currently account for about 50 percent of the country's net balance of trade. The realities of a global economy can only lend strength to their bargaining position and, at the same time, under arrangements such as the Canada/U.S. Free Trade Agreement, give governments less regulatory power.

"Major corporations... have invested millions of dollars in convincing the public that they really *are* good corporate citizens. At the same time, they lobby government to ensure that regulations do not jeopardize corporate profits."

Canadian pulp and paper industry lobbyists have also been successful federally in the face of declining profits. On February 1, 1991, Industry Minister Benoit Bouchard announced a reprieve for some companies in meeting new federal emission standards for dioxins, furans and suspended solids.

A globalized economy puts pressure on labor to accept less in order to allow TNCs operating in Canada to compete with their foreign counterparts. TNCs also claim that accepting less is necessary to keep the corporation in question operating within Canadian borders and to prevent a major relocation to another part of the world where labor is cheap.

TNCs and the globalization of the economy have put pressure on governments to introduce policies which will reduce both the environmental and social costs of production. Governments are thus caught between conflicting pressures: corporate interests constantly reminding governments of global competitive pressures on the one hand, and a public which is demanding that governments get tough on industrial polluters on the other. Canadians also want to protect social programs which corporate interests would like to see reduced or curtailed in order to reduce government deficits, corporate taxes and interest rates.

The result has been an incredible binge of public relations exercises. Major corporations—such as those in the forest industry represented by the Council of Forest Industries—have invested millions of dollars in convincing the public that they really *are* good corporate citizens. At the same time, they lobby government to ensure that regulations do not jeopardize corporate profits. In response to these pressures, government has often attempted to have it both ways—to appease public demands and corporate demands by paying, from general revenues, the costs of industry meeting new standards. Thus corporations have been given government grants, interest-free loans, government loan guarantees and other incentives.

Coupled with the pressure to minimize corporate taxation, the result has been a contribution to fiscal deficits. In turn, these deficits are blamed by the corporate sector on the cost of Canada's so-called welfare state. The private sector calls for an end of universal social programs and changes to others. But directly and indirectly, Canadian corporate interests are the largest recipients of government largesse and hence the most obvious contributors to the federal deficit. In B.C., the forest company Canfor received a government interest-free loan of $43 million in 1990 for the production of wood-fibre composite mats at its plant in New Westminster. Canfor had net incomes of $102.7 million, $101.6 million and $96.4 million in 1987, 1988, and 1989 respectively.

The growing competition and conflict between corporate interests and working people in Canada is likely to make the issue of who controls the media more critical. Both major daily papers in Vancouver are owned by Southam Press, a Toronto-based company which recently purchased 14 community newspapers, giving it an effective monopoly in the Lower Mainland.

In addition to using political influence, TNCs act in a number of other ways to minimize the costs incurred in meeting the social and environmental price of their activities. These include: disputing the scientific findings on which regulation may be based; threatening to close down an operation and/or to relocate or not to invest unless concessions are granted; and positioning themselves in regard to a regional population in order to enhance dependent relations with the community in question.

Owning And Disputing The Facts

Disputing the facts is easier to do for TNCs, many of which have research and development budgets which rival those of many North American universities. Money means the ability to buy expertise, endow universities—seen by the public to produce ideas and research uncontaminated by vested interests—and even to generate the data upon which environmental control decisions are based.

Dr. David Strangway, for example, President of the University of British Columbia, should perhaps be better known as a significant shareholder in the forest company MacMillan Bloedel (MB) and, even more significantly, as an active member of its board of directors (sitting on MB's audit, nominating, donations and environmental committees). It is no surprise that funds from the forest industry and its affiliates regularly find their way on to campus. Environmentalists will recognize Dr. Strangway as the University President who chaired a government committee which set up the B.C. Round Table on the Environment. No conflict of interest there!

Part of the logic of free trade and globalization involves reducing the costs and the role of government in the ordering of public affairs. In Canada, as the federal government cuts back on funds for research by Environment Canada and on funds available to universities, as research is increasingly privatized, sources of information to counter the biases of forest and other corporate interests are reduced. For example:

> "There is no scientific consensus about how much dioxin is too much for humans. Ron Woznow, Vice President of the Environment at Fletcher Challenge Canada, says that "research shows no risk to human health from dioxins—especially in the minute quantities detected in pulp mill effluent." But others such as Dr. Francis Law, an environmental toxicologist at Simon Fraser Univeristy, caution that dioxins in fatty tissue could mean long-term, cancer-causing harm to humans."—*British Columbia Report*, July 16, 1990.

When Fletcher Challenge becomes a source of funding for the kind of research done by Dr. Francis, what will the results be and how will they be reported? British Columbians, like all Canadians, are caught in a battle for the public mind.

Facts are further confused by the regulatory process. Where corporations are responsible for self-monitoring, the results are entirely predictable. What gets reported, and how, is very much a matter of corporate discretion. This problem has plagued the regulation of pulp mills in B.C., as revealed by the case of the Western Canada Forest Products mill near Squamish, when the company failed, in June of 1990, to report a fourfold increase in dioxins in the plant's effluent. (*British Columbia Report*, June 25, 1990.)

The Threat Of Closure

The elimination of barriers to trade increases the mobility of transnational interests. If a corporation no longer has to worry about tariff barriers to get its product into a country, then it can leave the nation in question, manufacture its product elsewhere and ship it back without penalty. Globalization has added new leverage to the threat of plant closure by TNCs.

B.C.-based TNCs have used this ploy in attempts to secure concessions around environmental regulation and controls. The setting aside of half of the Carmanah Valley as a provincial park, and the proposed emission standards for MacMillan Bloedel's mill in Port Alberni, prompted Noranda Forest Products (owners of MB) to send 200 of its workers at the Alberni pulp operations a letter notifying them that they will be looking for new jobs in 1992. The company claimed that environmental demands had created too much uncertainty to warrant new investment.

Dependent Relations

In rural areas, it is often the case that entire communities and regions are dependent for their economic and social survival on one employer and that employer may be a TNC whose commitment to the local community is constrained by the profitability concerns of corporate headquarters in Toronto, New York or Tokyo.

Dependency severely restricts the extent to which a community or a region can exercise responsibility for its own future. Many Canadian communities and residents of resource towns are, therefore, understandably careful about how they respond to the corporate presence in their community. Where the labor force is strongly unionized, corporations also play the role of good corporate citizen, making funds and facilities available for hockey clubs, senior citizens, etc. Criticism is often muted accordingly. Foundation grants as well as government funding can therefore be regarded as an effective means of social control.

Where infrastructure—including water, electricity and waste management—is minimal or non-existent, corporations sometimes become the source of these services. The municipality of Campbell River, B.C., is currently considering hooking its sewage treatment up to a new secondary treatment facility being built to serve the nearby Fletcher Challenge pulp mill. Campbell River currently has limited primary treatment. During the wet winter months, much sewage bypasses even this minimal treatment and is discharged directly into the Strait of Georgia. The volume of sewage originating with the municipality would be about three to four percent of the total volume treated by the company's facility.

This solution is clearly better than the existing alternative and has already been tried in the case of Quesnel and Cariboo Pulp and Paper in the interior. However, what are the long-term implications of this association between the municipality and the mill? Is it possible, were federal water quality standards to change in light of new information on the environmental effects of pulp mill discharges, that the relationship to the community might be used in bargaining with Environment Canada? How does municipal dependence on the facility affect labor relations at the mill?

The Need For A Common Analysis

Increasingly, a wholistic analysis is essential to acting locally and acting effectively. Unfortunately, many interest groups which should and must work together to address the issues outlined here are incapable of doing so.

Much of the problem lies with lack of a common analysis among groups addressing corporate power. Consistent with western culture, environmentalists and trade unionists alike tend to compartmentalize problems and approaches. Environmental issues are not "single issues," and to pretend otherwise is to undermine dealing with them effectively. Social conditions and environmental quality are the same thing to corporate interests: they are an expense. The same reasons that explain opposition to tough standards for the discharge of organochlorines into B.C. coastal waters explain corporate support for free trade and opposition to universal daycare or family allowances. We need coalitions of people who see the relationship between environmental and social conditions and the corporate agenda. A common analysis and appreciation of how our interests are joined is essential to effective social and political action.

"A common analysis and appreciation of how our interests are joined is essential to effective social and political action."

We need, at federal and provincial levels, governments which appreciate where the current dynamics of world power and corporate activity are taking us. We need governments which are critical of both market logic and the alternative conventions of central planning within a social democratic state. We need governments which will move to redress the serious imbalance in power between the corporate sector and the state. The abandonment of control over social and economic affairs to the market means the loss of social programs as well as increasing difficulty in dealing with environmental problems. We must replace existing political regimes with alternatives which are not allied with corporate power.

While decentralization and greater community control may be an alternative and progressive form of political expression, these options require closer examination. It is not clear that community control alone will be effective in countering the political and economic power of TNCs. The details of how regional and community control of resources might work in addressing the situations just described require close scrutiny.

Part Two

Small Ideas:
Conceiving Of Community
Control

To believe in community control is to be able to imagine a different kind of power than that wielded by mega-corporations and governments over people and place. The ideas presented in the following pages deal with the power of people to create and maintain cooperative, self-governing relations with one another in a democratic and ecologically sustainable fashion. Many "small" ideas need consideration, since their consequences are large—indeed, our survival may depend upon the strategies they suggest. For the well-being of the "whole"—this wonderous blue-green planet—is totally dependent on the parts: a vast array of symbiotic communities.

3

"Free And Equal Intercourse:" The Decentralist Design

Kirkpatrick Sale

Community self-government is not merely a new political idea. On the contrary, it is the very basis of all biological life. When humankind is seen as part of nature, instead of somehow separate and "above" nature, the demand for empowerment at a local level can be appreciated as a vital attempt to restore our relationship to our evolutionary origins.

Kirkpatrick Sale is a founding member of the North American Bioregional Congress and of the Hudson Bioregional Congress and its Wetlands Restoration Project. The author of six books, including Dwellers In the Land: The Bioregional Vision *and, most recently,* The Conquest of Paradise: Christopher Columbus and the Columbian Legacy, *he provides here the "natural history" of the decentralist idea.*

We find no boss in the brain, no oligarchic ganglion or glandular Big Brother. Within our heads our very lives depend on equality of opportunity, on specialisation with versatility, on free communication and just restraint, a freedom without interference. Here too, local minorities can and do control their own means of production and expression in free and equal intercourse with their neighbours. — Gary Walter, neurologist.

Inasmuch as bioregional designs and institutions take their shape from those principles of nature that enunciate themselves in healthy and fruitful ecosystems, it seems inevitable that a bioregional polity would be essentially based upon the universal phenomenon of *decentralism*: the devolution of power to small, mainly cooperative, and largely equivalent units.

This is the universal pattern in the natural world, where nothing is more striking than the absence of any centralized control, any interspeciate domination, where there are none of the patterns of ruler-and-ruled that are taken as inevitable in human governance. "King of the jungle" is *our* description of the lion's status, and quite anthropomorphously perverse; the lion (or, better, lioness) is profoundly unaware of this role, and the elephant and rhinoceros (not to mention the tsetse fly) would hardly accede to it. In a biotic community the various sets of animals and plants, no matter how they may run their own families and clusters, behave smoothly and regularly with each other without the need of any overall system of authority or dominance, any biotic Washington or Wall Street, in fact without any governing organization or superstructure of any kind whatsoever. No one species rules over all—or any—others, not one even makes the attempt, not one even has either instinct or intention in that direction. (Even the kudzu and the redtide bacteria, for all that they sometimes look as if they have in mind to conquer the world, are merely blindly moving into comfortable new environments and have no thought of rule or enslavement.)

"in the natural world...nothing is more striking than the absence of any centralized control, any interspeciate domination, ...there are none of the patterns of ruler-and-ruled that are taken as inevitable in human governance."

What's more, when several subgroups of a single species occupy the same region, there is no attempt to consolidate power in one of them: you never see one colony of crows try to conquer another, one pride of lions try to establish control over all the other lions around. *Territoriality*, yes: often a subgroup of a species attempts to carve out a niche in the ecosystem for itself and goes to considerable lengths to keep other members of that species (and competing species) away. But that is not governance, not the creation of any central authority, it is merely a familial or communal statement about the carrying capacity of that niche for that species—and, I guess, of who was there first to measure it. And *defense*, too: there can be quite intense and deadly conflict when one subgroup defends its home—hive or hill, roost or lair—from another, and mammalian familes and individuals will often go to great lengths, including aggression at times, to protect females and their young during birth and nesting periods. But these are not battles of conquest, they are not followed by domination or colonization (though some ants will take other ants as prisoners), and they are never caused by one subgroup desiring to establish its rule, its command, over another.

Now there is, of course, one continuous exercise of power between species in the ecosphere: many animals perforce depend on ingesting other animals and a wide range of plants. There is in fact a regular practice we call *predation* by which certain species live in a quasi-symbiotic relationship of hunter and hunted, eater and eaten, and it is common among all biotic communities and among many species of animals as well as a few plants. But this is not governance, it is not rule or dominance, it is not even aggression of an organized political or military kind. The predatory relationship is certainly one of violence and death (and sustenance and life), certainly one of imbalance and non-reciprocation, but it is never undertaken for anything but food—not for governance, or control, or the establishment of power or sovereignty. An exercise of power it is, but it is still diffused power, almost *accidental* power. (Moreover, there is always some kind of mutuality at work in predation, even though it is of an unconscious kind and may go quite unappreciated by the prey; one could not really expect the caribou to welcome the attack by the gray wolf pack, though in fact it is a necessary means of controlling the herd's population, and by weaning out the weakest and sickest helps to strengthen the herd's genetic heritage.)

*

A similar kind of decentralism, a recurrent urge toward separatism, independence, and local autonomy rather than agglomeration and concentration, exists in human patterns as well. Throughout all human history, even in the past several hundred years, people have tended to live in separate and independent small groups, a "fragmentation of human society" that Harold Isaacs, the venerated professor of international affairs at MIT, has described as something akin to "a pervasive force in human affairs." Even when nations and empires have arisen, he notes, they have no staying power against the innate human drive toward decentralism:

> The record shows that there could be all kinds of lags, that declines could take a long time and falls run long overdue, but that these conditions could never be indefinitely maintained. Under external or internal pressures—usually both—authority was eroded, legitimacy challenged, and in wars, collapse, and revolution, the system of power redrawn.

Propaganda of the nation-state to the contrary, once you begin to re-read history with an attention to this persistence of the decentralist impetus you begin to see everywhere that the existence of the anti-authoritarian, independent, self-regulating, local community is every bit as basic to the human record as the existence of the centralized, imperial, hierarchical state—and far more ancient, more durable, and more widespread.

Obviously for the three million years that humanoids were becoming human, they lived in small clans and groups, and for the next 10,000 years that they were becoming "civilized" they lived in small communities and towns, needing none but the most limited kinds of governmental structures. Throughout the era of oriental empires—Persian, Sumerian, Egyptian, Babylonian—the greater part of the world's people still lived in independent hamlets, ever resistant to the imposition of outside authority, and even within the empires themselves local self-governing communes always persisted. Later, the Essenes, the people of the Dead Sea Scrolls who established an egalitarian community in opposition to Romanic Jerusalem in the second century before Christ, were only one of myriad tribes and sects that lived deliberately outside the Roman imperial influence. And still later the Christians themselves often lived in democratic and independent communities, sometimes in secret and sometimes openly but always apart from and hostile to whatever state might claim sovereignty.

"for the three million years that humanoids were becoming human, they lived in small clans and groups, and for the next 10,000 years that they were becoming "civilized" they lived in small communities and towns, needing none but the most limited kinds of governmental structures."

The settlements of Greece were typical of such resistant localism: for many centuries they clung to a fierce independence, city upon city, valley after valley, no matter what putative conquerors might intrude, in time achieving that Hellenic civilization that is still a marvel of the world. As historian Rudolf Rocker has written of them:

> Greece was politically the most dismembered country on earth. Every city took zealous care lest its political independence be assailed; for this the inhabitants of even the smallest of them were in no mind to surrender. Each of these little city-republics had its own constitution, its own social life with its own cultural peculiarities; and this it was that gave to Hellenic life as a whole its variegated wealth of genuine cultural values.

> It was this healthy decentralization, this internal separation of Greece into hundreds of little communities, tolerating no uniformity, which constantly aroused the mind to consideration of new matters. Every larger political structure leads inevitably to a certain rigidity of the cultural life

and destroys that fruitful rivalry between separate communities which is so characteristic of the whole life of the Grecian cities.

Even to call it "Greece" is indeed to employ a modern fiction: the citizens of that ancient culture thought of themselves as Athenians and Spartans and Thebans, not Greeks, alike in language and civilization but not in political stamp or rule.

Traditional historians write of the European period from the fall of Rome to the Renaissance as if nothing much were going on outside of the consolidation of feudal families into the monarchies of the sub-sequent nation-states. But that is like talking of the night as the presence of stars or the ocean as if it were only waves. What was going on throughout the continent from the Atlantic to the Urals, what kept European civilization alive for better than ten centuries, was the main-tenance and development of small, independent communities—here in the form of Teutonic and Russian and Saxon villages with their popular councils and judicial elders, there as the medieval city-states with their guilds and brotherhoods and folkmotes, and over there as the chartered towns which spread by the hundreds over France and Belgium with their special instruments of sovereignty and self-jurisdiction. Chracteristic of the look of the continent were the divided cantons of what became Switzerland, which began with the first democratic commune in Uri in the 1230s and became a form that spread through dozens of villages in the fourteenth and fifteenth centuries and lasted until dominance by Napoleon at the end of the eighteenth century. The independent Swiss Republic of the Three Leagues, at its height a typical canton covering an area about the size of Dallas, consisted of three loosely federated leagues, 26 sub-jurisdictions, 49 jurisdictional communes, and 227 autonomous neighborhoods—and, as an eighteenth-century traveler put it, "each village…each parish and each neighbourhood already constituted a tiny republic."

That Europe did eventually evolve some families designating them-selves royal, and that some of those conquered vast areas of land they liked to call nations, and that the whole became a system of border-drawn nation-states such as we know today, does not mean that this was the tide and trend of that long era. Indeed, as between the statist tradition and the decentralist, these thousand years were clearly the period of the latter, into the fifteenth century in western European territories, in some places into the nineteenth century in eastern. No one understood this period better than the Russian scientist and anarchist Peter Kropotkin, whose careful researches into its long-neglected intricacies, built upon the absolute explosion of interest in village government by scholars everywhere in the nineteenth century, have given us a telling picture of those centuries:

> Self-jurisdiction was the essential point [of the commune] and self-juris-diction meant self-administration.... It had the right of war and peace, of federation and alliance with its neighbors. It was sovereign in its own affairs, and mixed with no others.

> In all its affairs the village commune was sovereign. Local custom was the law, and the plenary assembly of all the heads of family—men and women—was the judge, the only judge, in civil and criminal matters....

> [In medieval towns] each street or parish had its popular assembly, its forum, its popular tribunal, its priest, its militia, its banner, and often its seal, the symbol of its sovereignty. Though federated with other streets it nevertheless maintained its independence.

This was the rule, mind, not the exception; it was exactly this self-governing community, through pestilence and war, the vicissitudes of nature and of kings, that sustained the many tens of millions of people of Europe for a millennium and more.

Nor did the tradition end with the rise of the nation-state. In many places it persisted for quite a time—France did not outlaw local folkmotes until 1789, and Russian communes continued to exist in countless places until finally gutted by Stalin as late as the 1930s. Even in the age of nationalism it is not difficult to find, just below the surface, the roughly independent peasant village, the headstrong town, the self-minding neighborhood, in almost any country of Europe.

*

The lessons, then, from the natural world as from human history, seem to be clear enough. Bioregional polities as they evolve would seek the maximum diffusion of power and decentralization of institutions, with nothing done at a level higher than necessary, and all authority flowing upward incrementally from the smallest political unit to the largest.

The primary location of decision-making, therefore, and of political and economic control, should be the community, the more-or-less intimate grouping either at the close-knit village scale of 1,000 people or so, or probably more often at the extended community scale of 5,000 to 10,000 so often found as the fundamental political unit whether formal or informal. Here, where people know one another and the essentials of the environment they share, where at least the most basic information for problem-solving is known or readily available, here is where governance should begin. Decisions made at this level, as countless eons testify, stand at least a fair chance of being correct and a reasonable likelihood of being carried out competently; and even if the choice is misguided or the implementation faulty, the damage to either the society or the ecosphere is likely to be insignificant. This is the sort of government established by preliterate peoples all over the globe, evolving over the years toward a kind of bedrock efficiency in problem-solving simply because it was necessary for survival. In the tribal councils, the folkmotes, the ecclesia, the village assemblies, the town meetings, we find the human institution proven through time to have shown the scope and competence for the most basic kind of self-rule.

"What kept European civilization alive for better than ten centuries was the maintenance and development of small, independent communities."

As different species live side by side in an ecosystem, so different communities could live side by side in a single city, and cities and towns side by side in a single bioregion, with no more thought of dominance and control than the sparrow gives to the rose, or the bobcat to the wasp. Sharing the same bioregion, they naturally share the same configurations of life, the same social and economic constraints, roughly the same environmental problems and opportunities, and so there is every reason to expect contact and cooperation among them, for some specific tasks, maybe even confederation among them—but of a kind that need not mean diminished power or sovereignty for the community, but rather enlarged horizons of knowledge, of culture, of services, of security.

Of course communities with a bioregional consciousness would find countless occasions that called for regional cooperation—and decision-making—on all sorts of issues from water and waste management, transportation, and food production to upstream pollution seeping into downstream drinking water and urban populations moving into rural farming country. Isolationism and self-sufficiency at a local scale is simply impossible, like fingers trying to be independent of hand and body. Communication and information networks of all kinds would be—would need to be—maintained among the communities of a bioregion, and possibly some kind of political deliberative and decision-making body would eventually seem to be necessary.

The forms for such confederate bodies are myriad and their experiences rich and well-documented, so presumably working out the various systems would not be intractably difficult. A confederation within bioregional limits has the logic, the force, of coherence and commonality;

a confederation beyond those limits does not. Any larger political form is not only superfluous, it stands every chance of being downright dangerous, particularly since it is no longer organically grounded in an ecological identity or limited by the constraints of homogeneous communities.

If, as the scholars suggest, the goal of government as we have now come to understand it in the 20th century is to provide liberty, equality, efficiency, welfare, and security in some reasonable balance, a strong argument can be made that it is the *spatial* division of power, divided and subdivided again as in bioregional governance, that provides them best. It promotes *liberty* by diminishing the chances of arbitrary government action and providing more points of access for the citizens, more points of pressure for affected minorities. It enhances *equality* by assuring more participation by individuals and less concentration of power in a few remote and unresponsive bodies and offices. It increases *efficiency* by allowing government to be more sensitive and flexible, recognizing and adjusting to new conditions, new demands from the populace it serves. It advances *welfare* because at the smaller scales it is able to measure people's needs best and to provide for them more quickly, more cheaply, and more accurately. And, because of all that, it actually improves *security* because unlike the big and bumbling megastates vulnerable to instability and alienation, it fosters the sort of cohesiveness and allegiance that discourages crime and disruption within and discourages aggression and attack from without.

The visioning and formulation of a bioregional polity does nothing in itself, however, to assure that such a future evolves. But I think there is real and pertinent wisdom in E.F. Schumacher's remark that "only if we *know* that we have actually descended into *infernal regions*"—and who would want to deny that that is the present condition of the industrial world?—"can we summon the courage and imagination needed for a 'turning around,' a *metanoia*." *Once knowing that—knowing* that—we may then see "the world in a new light, namely, as a place where the things modern man continuously talks about and always fails to accomplish *can actually be done.*"

That, at any rate, is our only hope. What other choice, really, do we have?

4

The Best Government Comes In Small Packages

John Papworth

"The bigger, the better" is perhaps the single most destructive idea of our times, especially when it comes to the institutions of government. Obsessed with the fallacy of economies of scale, modern societies groan beneath the burden of over-blown bureaucracies and a disempowered citizenry. Curiously, proposed solutions to our ills frequently involve yet larger and more centralized institutional forms.

Going against this trend for some 25 years has been the Fourth World movement—a somewhat obscure but international network of those favoring "small nations, small communities and the human spirit." John Papworth, an Anglican priest from London, England, has been a prime mover and shaker of the Fourth World, convening annual Assemblies and editing The Fourth World Review.

Nothing is real unless it is local, quipped G. K. Chesterton, the British novelist and political philosopher. If Chesterton is correct, government in the 20th century is extremely unreal.

To be "real," it is doubtful if any local area of government ought to exceed 5,000 people. This appears to be about the maximum number that enables local people to have an involvement in local problems, and to achieve the kind of interaction that enables them to solve these problems.

True democracy is only possible when people have effective power over their own affairs, their own goals, and their own resources. The larger the governing unit, the less responsive it is to human needs, the more bureaucratic and inefficient its administration. Government, we must always remind ourselves, is not (or should not be) a professionally

28

organized system to tell people how to run their affairs; it is (or should be) a means whereby people themselves are enabled to resolve matters in their own community. A local unit of government that begins to grow significantly beyond 5,000 persons begins to be less "local," and there emerges a need for more professional people to manage affairs that in a smaller community people are able to manage for themselves.

The major justification for the enlargement of local government units is that they are cheaper and more efficient to run. Yet anyone who still has any lingering illusions about the efficiency of giant schools, hospitals, and police forces over small local ones is simply not keeping abreast of modern life as reported in our daily newspapers.

It is still frequently argued that small, local communities cannot "afford" to run such services. Any suggestion that they might do so is at once countered by the seemingly unanswerable question, "Where is the money to come from?" The obvious reply should be: "From where it is now going." It is now going to fund vast centralized bureaucracies. If a local community ran its own affairs (by which I mean its schools, hospitals, police, housing, welfare, and other local services), and if central government ran only those concerns that can be described as truly national (such as defense, foreign affairs, the judiciary, and so on), then central government would require far less money.

"It is doubtful any area of local goverment ought to exceed 5,000 people. "

Another justification of centralized government is that the revenues are used to ensure some equality between rich and poor. Any discussion about the localization of government sooner or later raises the question of how poor localities are going to manage compared with rich ones. Nobody wants to see poor localities left to stew in their own juices, but we need to ask why they are poor in the first place. And why, for that matter, if the idea of central government was working, are the poor areas still poor?

These questions gain in pertinence when we recall that many of the areas now being described as poor are the ones in which much of the material wealth of the world has been produced. What then has happened to the wealth? Let's look at Britain as an example. Under the impact of increasingly centralized forms of government, there has been a steady drain of wealth and power away from the north to the south and especially to London. This has led to other forms of impoverishment such as a "brain drain," a drain of talents and abilities away from the north.

People of talent and ability will normally tend to gravitate to places where their talents are used and their abilities recognized; this means they will gravitate to where the decisions are made and where funding for their projects and careers is likely to be found. Increasingly the magnetic pull of London, the over-centralized British capital and the center of decision-making, wealth, influence, communication, opportunity, and recognition, proves irresistible.

The cultural scene tells its own story. In London, in any one evening, there will be more than 50 live theater performances from which to choose. It is worth noting that few provincial cities can boast more than one theater, which generally has to struggle to survive at all. Yet why should this be? Why cannot Birmingham, for example, with its two and a half million population in northern England, representing more than one third of the population of greater London, not be able to boast of at least one third of the number of London's live theaters?

The answer is to be found in the little-recognized fact that centralization creates poverty. One person who has recognized this fact is Professor Leopold Kohr, who was the first to propound "the law of peripheral neglect," which states that the further a place is from the government and economic centers, the poorer it is likely to be. So if Wales and Scotland are poor in relation to greater London (despite their superiority of natural resources), so too are Sardinia, Sicily, and the Italian south in relation to Rome and Milan, and the American South and Midwest in relation to Washington, New York, and Los Angeles.

How does this come about? To find out, we need only look at what actually happens in the economic sphere. A community of 5,000 people that was largely self-governing and largely economically self-sufficient would presumably have established itself and developed on the basis of some natural resources. If this community provides most of its needs from its own resources, it would have a basis on which to advance to prosperity. If, however, it comes to rely on others for most of its basic needs, it will simply be providing a basis for the prosperity of others.

This holds true even if it produces a considerable amount of products or raw materials for export. Why then is the value of its own exports not sufficient to enrich it and enable it to use such riches to enhance its prosperity? The answer is to be found in the fact that trade is conducted on certain terms, and the small community is generally in no position to ensure that those terms will be favorable to itself. Hence for a community to engage in trade it must also surrender some of its power. And the more it depends on trade, the *less* it is able to depend on itself.

If, for example, a family sits down to a breakfast of bread made from the wheat grown in local fields, butter and milk produced by local cows, and honey from local bees, it will accomplish a number of specific goals—not least of which will be asserting a measure of economic and political independence, and helping to enrich both itself and its community. If the family produces the food itself, it will save money with which to enrich itself in other ways; if it buys food from neighbors who have produced it, it is helping to generate local incomes and local employment. It is not difficult to see how this process is further enhanced if the local bank is locally owned (especially by the community as a whole) so that the profits of banking and credit are also retained for local enrichment.

Yet what happens if the same family decides to breakfast on, let us say, a packaged cereal, sugar from Malawi, and coffee from Kenya? It at once becomes part of a complex web of international trading relationships, the workings of which inevitably proceed to impoverish not only the family but the local community as a whole. This results in a considerable decline of the community's political and economic power, which is transferred to remote centers of commerce. These centers will then proceed to use that power to further enhance their own dominance.

We may see this situation more clearly if we assume that the local wealth of this community is retained by local people and is used to develop local resources and local skills. On these terms, the economic surplus would be available to the local community. Its own members would thus decide, on the basis of their knowledge of local resources and local needs, how it should be used. A community that beautified its buildings, built a fine theater and concert hall, and produced high-quality local products, for example, would find itself becoming a magnet for its own talents as well as those of others, rather than being a boring backwater of social stagnation.

5

Dis-Union Now!

Leopold Kohr

Flying in the face of nature, human forms of governance in both ancient and modern times have tended inexorably toward hugeness of scale. But the fact that empires have not endured over time seems rarely to have been sufficiently acknowledged. Ironically, the happy dismantling of the Berlin Wall is followed by the dubious reunification of Germany and the building of another huge European power bloc—a mere switch from one disproportionately vast government to another. The mania for giant forms of "unity" continues its patently destructive and impoverishing course.

Yet half a century ago, one lone voice was proclaiming a different truth, the relevance of which has become increasingly urgent with the passage of time and which marks him out as one of the prophetic voices of the modern era. Leopold Kohr—the Austrian author of The Breakdown Of Nations, *a book which was a major influence on E.F. Schumacher—has argued for years that giantism is the cause of our governing problems. This article was first published in 1941 in* The Commonweal.

We like to believe that the misery into which the world has come is due to the fact that humanity is split into too many countries. And we like to believe that all the evils of our globe would be eliminated by simply doing away with the variety of states through uniting—the democracies now, the continents later, the world in the end. The usually-cited examples for the feasibility of such unions are the United States of America and Switzerland.

As far as the United States is concerned, it is not a model after which Europe could be reshaped because it is not a union of different entities. There is no real differentiation between the peoples, languages, customs and races living in the various states. There is only one people, the American, living in the United States, which is plural in its name but not in fact. The United States *are* not a country, it *is* a country. The only lesson which can be drawn from its constitutional picture is that, in spite of the uniformity of type it has produced, it was found more practicable to subdivide it into 48 states instead of trying to govern the entire continent through delegates from Washington. Thus differentiations were artificially created because this proved to be an easier way to achieve union than unification.

But more than the United States, it is Switzerland which is regarded as the proof of the feasibility of the unionist dreams, even for the continent of Europe where they have neither a uniform type of continental person, nor a common language, nor a common cultural and historical background. There, in a tiny spot in the Alps, three arch-enemies—Italians, Germans and French— have united for the common purpose of freedom, peace and economic happiness. Switzerland, to the unionist, is the eternal example of the practicability of the living together of different nations, and, for this reason, is praised as a holy land.

"The greatness of the Swiss idea, therefore, is the smallness of its cells from which it derives its guarantees."

But in reality Switzerland, too, proves something quite different from what she is meant to prove. The percentage of her national groups (not speaking of the Romanche, her fourth nationality) is roughly 70 percent for the German, 20 percent for the French and 10 percent for the Italian-speaking population. If these three national groups as such were the basis of her much-famed union, it would inevitably result in the domination of the large German- speaking block over the other two nationalities, who would become degraded to the logical status of minorities representing only 30 percent of the total population. Indeed, the rules of democracy would favour this development, and the reason for the French- and Italian-speaking communities remaining in a chiefly German enterprise would be gone. No sense could be found in their keeping away from the more logical union with their own blood-relatives who, through their number, have formed the powerful nations of Italy and France. No more sense could there be for the Germanic block to stay outside the Reich.

In fact the basis of the existence of Switzerland and the principle of living together of various national groups is not the federation of her three nationalities but the federation of her 22 states, which represent a division of her nationalities and thus create the essential precondition for any democratic federation: the physical balance of the participants, the approximate equality of numbers. The greatness of the Swiss idea, therefore, is the smallness of its cells from which it derives its guarantees. The Swiss from Geneva does not confront the Swiss from Zurich as a French to a German confederate, but as a confederate from the Republic of Geneva to a confederate from the Republic of Zurich. The citizen of German-speaking Uri is as much a foreigner to the citizen of German-speaking Unterwalden as he is to the citizen of Italian-speaking Tessin. Between the canton of St. Gallen and the Swiss federation is no inter-mediary organization in the form of "German-speaking cantons." The power delegated to Berne derives from the small member republic and not from the nationality, because Switzerland is a union of states, not of nations.

It is important to realise that in Switzerland there live (in rough numbers) 700,000 Bernese; 650,000 Zurichois; 160,000 Genevese; etc; and not 2,500,000 Germans; 1,000,000 French and 500,000 Italians. The great number of proud, democratic and almost sovereign cantons, and the small number of the individual cantonal populations eliminates all possible imperialist ambitions on the part of any one canton, because it would always be outnumbered by even a very small combination of others. If ever, in the course of contemporary simplification and rationalisation, an attempt to reorganise Switzerland on the basis of its nationalities should succeed, the 22 "superfluous" states with all their separate parliaments and governments would become three provinces: not of Switzerland, however, but of Germany, Italy and France.

Cantonal Sovereignty

People who argue for a union of nations in Europe because they believe that this kind of union has been realised and thus proved its practicability in Switzerland, have never based their wonderful schemes on the principle of cantonal or small-state sovereignty. The *national* idea has so much troubled the minds of the political thinkers that, in contrast, the notion of *state*, which is so much more flexible, adaptable and multipliable than that of *nation*, has almost completely gone out of use. For virtue has been seen only in great and greater entities, while smaller entities have been thought and taught to be the source of all mischief and evil. We have been educated in the worship of the bulk, of the large, of the universal, of the colossal, and have come away from the miniscule, the completeness and universality on the smallest scale—the individual, which is the protoplasm of all social life. We have learned to praise the unification of France, Britain, Italy and Germany in the belief that they would give birth to a unified humanity. But they created only Great Powers.

If the Swiss experience should be applied to Europe, the Swiss technique—not merely the appearance of its result—will also have to be employed. This consists in the dividing of three or any number of unequal blocks into as many smaller parts as is necessary to eliminate any sizeable numerical preponderance. That is to say that one should create 40 or 50 equally small states instead of four or five unequally large ones. Otherwise even a federated Europe will always contain 80 million Germans, 45 million French, 45 million Italians, etc., which means that any European federation would end up in a German hegemony with just the same inevitablity as the German federation, in which 24 small states were linked to the one 40-million Power of Prussia, ended up in Prussian hegemony.

The suggestion, therefore, is to split Germany up into a number of states of seven to ten million inhabitants. This could be easily done since the former German states (or a number of them) could be reconstructed, and even Prussia could be divided on a natural and historic basis. The splitting up of Germany alone, however, would have no permanent effect. With the natural tendency of all growing things, Germany would reunite unless the whole of Europe were to be cantonised at the same time. France, Italy and Russia must be divided too. Also, in their cases, their historical backgrounds would make the task easy; we shall again have a Venezia, a Lombardy, a Burgundy, a Savoy, an Esthonia, a White Russia, etc. But as with the German states, here also the new (or old) entities would again grow together on racial lines unless they are brought together in new combinations, making the creation of national states impossible. That is to say, the true meaning of Switzerland or the Austro-Hungarian Empire will have to be realized in many new instances: the small states should be federated, but not with their nearest relative, so that the new map of Europe might show a Pomerania-West Poland, an East-Prussia-Baltica, an Austria-Hungary-Czechoslovakia, a Baden-Burgundy, a Lombardy-Savoy, etc. Then the Great Powers, which are the womb of all modern wars, because they alone are strong enough to give to war its modern frightfulness, shall have disappeared. But only through splitting up the entire continent of Europe would it be possible to eliminate honorably Germany or any other great Power without having to inflict on any the odium of a new Versailles. Once Europe is divided into small enough parcels, we shall have the Swiss foundation of a Pan-European Union, based not on the collaboration of powerful nations, but on the smallness of all of the states.

Glorifying The Small

All this is a defence of the much ridiculed principle which glorifies the sovereignty of the smallest and not of the largest state-entity—*Kleinstaaterie*, as the Germans say. The theorists of our time who seem to be able to see only the large and get emotional over words like "humanity" (no one knows what it really means and why one should die for it) call the very idea of creating more, instead of fewer, states medieval backwardness. They are all in favor of unionism and colossalism, though unionism is nothing really but another expression for totalitarianism, even if it is thought to be a guarantee for peace. It is the one-party system transplanted into the international field.

Against the scorn of our theorists, I would like to point out only a very few of the advantages of this "medieval" scheme. The unionist will say that the time when hundreds of states existed was dark and that wars were waged almost continuously. That is true. But what were these wars like? The Duke of Tyrol declared war on the Margrave of Bavaria for a stolen horse. The war lasted two weeks. There was one dead and six wounded. A village was captured and all the wine drunk which was in the cellar of the inn. Peace was made and $35 was paid for reparations. The adjoining Duchy of Lichtenstein and the Archbishopric of Salzburg never learned that there had been a war at all. There was war in some corner of Europe almost every day, but these were wars with little effects. Today we have relatively few wars, and they are for no better reason than a stolen horse. But the effects are tremendous.

Also, economically, the advantages of the coexistence of many little states were enormous, although the modern synchronisers and economists will not agree with this, since they have got accustomed to seeing the world standing on their heads. Instead of one administration we had twenty, instead of two hundred parliamentarians we had two thousand and, thus, instead of the ambitions of only a few, the ambitions of many could be satisfied. There were no unemployed, because there were too many identical professions which competed *less* because they were exercised in *more* countries. There was no necessity for socialism (another totalitarian notion), because the economic life of a small country could be supervised from any church tower without the interpretations (brilliant though they be) of a Marx or Schacht. There was the development of the arts in the many capitals which excelled in the creation of universities, theatres and in the production of poets, philosophers and architects. And there were no more taxes than we have now, in the age of rationalisation, where people and enterprises have been "economised" for economic reasons and the phenomenon of unemployment has come into existence. We have done away with what we thought was the waste of courts and kings and have created thereby the splendour of the dictators' marching millions. We have ridiculed the many little states; now we are terrorised by their few successors.

Not only history, but also our own experience has taught us that true democracy in Europe can only be achieved in little states. Only there the individual can retain his place and dignity. And if democracy is a worthwhile idea, we have to create again the conditions for its development: the small state, and give the glory of sovereignty (instead of curtailing an institution from which no one wants to depart) to the smallest community and to as many as possible. It will be easy to unite small states under one continental federal system and thus also satisfy, secondarily, those who want to live on universal terms. Such a Europe is like a fertile inspiration and a grandiose picture, although not a modern one which you paint in one dull line. It will be like a mosaic with fascinating variations and diversity, but also with the harmony of the organic and living whole.

This is a ridiculous scheme, conceived for humankind as a witty, vivacious and individualistic reality. Unionism, on the other hand, is a deadly serious scheme without humor, meant for humanity as a collectivity and as social animals of lower order; and it reminds me constantly, in all its earnest elaborateness, of the German Professor who submitted to Satan a new plan for organizing Hell. Whereupon Satan answered with rock-shaking laughter: "Organize Hell? My dear Professor, organization is Hell."

6

From Roadblocks To Building Blocks: Developing A Theory For Putting Power In Its Place

Don Alexander

The demand for more local control has frequently been stimulated by communities suddenly facing the imposition of a toxic waste dump close by, or more clearcut logging in their watersheds, for example. Characterized as NIMBY—Not In My Back Yard—reactions, such responses are fully justified, but they often go little beyond the immediate concern. Consequently, communities remain divided in their calls for more local power and no long-term, integrated movement is created.

Don Alexander, a graduate student in the School of Urban and Regional Planning at the University of Waterloo, Ontario and co-chair of the Save The Oak Ridges Moraine (STORM) Coalition, believes that these isolated community actions could, if linked by more general theory, constitute a broader and more effective movement for putting more power in local places.

My own experience in working with citizens' groups in Ontario has led me to the conclusion that many of us are so busy putting out brushfires, and putting up roadblocks to development, that we never get around to thinking about what a sustainable society might look like, and how we might get there.

To do that we need a theory, and that's what we haven't got. A theory should tell us who are our *friends* and *enemies* or, to put it a different way, who favors change towards a sustainable society and who opposes it. It should tell us *what* needs to be changed, and it should tell us how to overcome *barriers* and take advantage of *opportunities*.

Friends And Enemies: The "Planetariat" And "Technocracy"

While it was once thought by Karl Marx that the main conflict in society was between workers and bosses, now many recognize that this is too simplistic—that some of the most important movements today are the peace, ecology, feminism, and pro-democracy movements. We have seen a growing together of these movements in what has been called the "green" movement.

Moreover, it's not just capitalism which is a problem. We have seen how governments and the scientific establishment have their own vested interest in supporting and driving forward the process of "development." I call this collaboration of business, government and science the "technocracy." The main goal of technocracy seems to be to dominate nature by taking away all its "intrinsic meaning and value, beauty and mystery" (Donald Worster), and seeking to control it through technology.

"To make peace with nature, society must emulate nature, at least in certain respects. It must become more self-regulating at the community level..."

Karl Marx saw the working class, or *proletariat*, as the leading agent of social change, and thought it would play a radical role because of its close involvement in the industrial process. I'm suggesting, in contrast with Marx, that the most radical group in society today is the "planetariat," which is largely *outside* the process of industrial production. The planetariat is partially in a *pre-* industrial position, and partially in a *post*-industrial position.

By *pre-industrial*, I mean Native peoples engaged in hunting, fishing, trapping, and horticulture. Also included here would be small farmers and fishermen engaged in production on a small scale. Even where the economic activities themselves have been absorbed into the world market economy, aspects of pre-industrial culture and values remain. By *post-industrial*, I'm referring to the growing importance of the service and professional sectors. This doesn't make industrial activity any less important, but it does make it less a part of people's everyday lives. Some have argued that those who are *not* directly involved in the industrial process—either as workers or managers—tend to be more critical of the industrial system, even while enjoying certain of its benefits.[1]

Marx thought that capitalism would drive the standard of living of the working class down to the point where its members would scarcely be able to survive, and that this would force rebellion. He called this "immiseration." By contrast, I see the technocracy creating *domestication*. I use the term in a very specific sense, following Murray Bookchin:

> In its own way, our loss of community has been a form of *domestication*—a condition that lacks meaning and direction.... Like our cattle, poultry, pets, and even crops, we too have lost our wildness in a "pacified" world that is overly administered and highly rationalized [emphasis added].—*The Ecology Of Freedom*, 1982.

This domestication is of three kinds: of nature (destruction and simplification of ecosystems), of politics (tendency to replace participation with bureaucracies), and of culture (to replace popularly-produced culture with "mass culture" and consumerism). Planetarians (to be defined shortly) often respond to the first kind, but, in so doing, come up against the other two kinds. Farley Mowat has described the conflict between the planetariat and the technocracy as follows:

> It is the conflict between those who possess the means and the will to exploit the living world to destruction and those who are banding together in a desperate and last-ditch attempt to prevent the New Juggernaut from trashing our small planet.
>
> If the right side wins, this combat may become known to future generations as the Crusade that Rescued the Earth. If the wrong side wins—there will be no future generations.
>
> The struggle is an unequal one. The Big Battalions belong to and are commanded by some of the most powerful individuals and cabals history ever recorded. Their battle cry is "Progress!" Their arsenals are supplied by Commerce and Industry. Their most fearsome weapon is Technology. Science is their supportive priesthood. Politics is their handmaiden.—Editorial, *Recover*, (Fall 1990).

The planetariat is a group defined by common values and a common worldview, although these are often not fully spelled out. At its heart are those who have a green or bioregional perspective. On the outer edge are people who are involved in "Not In My Back Yard" (NIMBY) struggles, but who have the potential to become concerned about much bigger issues. As I see it, the planetariat is made up of the following groups (with examples):

Indigenous Cultures:
• The Innu (Labrador);

- The Penan (Malaysia);
- The Yanomami (Brazil).

Folk or Agrarian Cultures:
- residual rural culture in farming communities in Canada, or fishing communities in the Maritimes and Newfoundland;
- peasant cultures in the "Third World" (the "Chipko" movement in India);
- "submerged nations" in Europe (Bretons, Basques, etc.).

"Counter-Cultures:"
- religious minorities (Quakers);
- back-to-the-landers and others (as in the bioregional movement);
- "humanistic intellectuals" (teachers, students) and educated professionals.

What They Have in Common:
- resistance to ecological, political, and cultural domestication;
- resistance to "development;"
- values counter-posed to those of industrialism.

Of crucial importance is the need to build an alliance between the rural sections of the planetariat (which tend to play a major role in front line battles against the destruction of ecosystems), and the urban sections (for instance, sympathetic artists, academics, and environmental activists) who, together with Native peoples, challenge cultural domestication and stress the need for planetary change. In this way, a movement which genuinely "thinks globally" and "acts locally" can be created.

The three kinds of domestication (ecological, political, and cultural) are related. The effort to dominate nature leads to a centralization of power, and a short-circuiting of the democratic process, as the nuclear industry demonstrates. Consumerism (a form of cultural domestication) is the bait that sucks people into supporting the domination of nature:

> [u]nder this project of [dominating nature], the individual's power over the natural environment (power realised in the form of wealth, comfort and gratification) increases remarkably, but... some people gain far more power than others.... Where wants and needs are out of self-control, where they cannot be defined and filled by the person and the immediate community, power must gravitate further and further away.[2]

Thus, resisting the values and culture of the technocracy is an integral part of resisting the degradation of nature and the bureaucratization of politics. Ultimately, the planetariat must go from merely *resisting* to creating new planetarian institutions. Institutions needing replacement include: *capitalism* (wage labor and production for profit), *statism* (bureaucratization of politics and centralization of authority), and *scientism* (seeing nature as "dead" stuff, along with the belief that issues of fact can be treated separately from issues of value).

What Needs To Be Changed: The "Mode Of Reproduction"

A basic framework for looking at contemporary problems is that every society can be described as a "mode of reproduction." Society is what enables us to be fulfilled materially, culturally, and spiritually, and this process is only sustainable when it happens in a way that is in relative harmony with natural systems. Societies change in their impacts as population and/or per capita consumption grow. Eventually a point is reached where a given mode of reproduction can no longer support human life without threatening the carrying capacity of the region, or indeed the biosphere as a whole. When that stage is reached, new values and institutions (and this includes different ways of making a living)— which jointly comprise a new mode of reproduction—must be sought to replace the old one. It is evident that we have reached this point in our own society.

In this respect, I find the accompanying chart useful in that it shows how the values and institutions of our present society contribute to a specific problem—urban sprawl—and how a different set of values and institutions might alleviate the problem.

Elements of a new mode would include changed attitudes towards nature, people, and self; forms of community and regional self-government—with equality and respect for women—and a synthesis of expert and vernacular knowledge; and a "communitarian" economy using ecologically and socially appropriate technology. The planetariat will potentially play an important role in helping to bring these institutions into existence. It represents a new mode while the technocracy represents the old.

Barriers And Opportunities: Ecological Democracy

There are three principles associated with "ecological democracy." The first is that democracy is essential to achieving peace with the planet. This has a number of parts to it. First of all, ordinary people tend to be more ecologically-minded than politicians and other members of the technocracy. Secondly, if a more ecological society is to be achieved without further victimizing the more vulnerable members of society, it is crucial that such groups be allowed—and indeed encouraged—to

KEY FEATURES OF SOCIETIES	PRESENT SOCIETY	AN ECOLOGICAL SOCIETY
(Different Parts of the Mode of Reproduction)	*(Factors contributing to "Urban Sprawl")*	*(Factors helping to eliminate "Urban Sprawl")*
VALUES:		
• *Attitudes towards nature*	—ecosystems as "raw land," as a mere factor in production	—seeing nature as a community of which we are only one member
• *Attitudes toward other people*	—extreme individualism; people have no ethical responsibilities to the community	—having responsibility to other people & future generations to use resources (farmland) wisely
• *Attitudes toward self*	—happiness equated with having possessions to be consumed in private	—self-realization in harmony with others more important than wealth
ORGANISATION:		
• *Political relations*	—gov't structures only superficially democratic, allowing control by development interests	—community/regional assemblies to plan sustainable use of resources
• *Cultural relations*	—dominance of "experts" who hide biases beneath a mantle of objectivity	—integration of local/indigenous knowledge into decision-making processes
• *Kinship relations*	—isolated nuclear families, each seeking to occupy its own private "castle"	—willingness to live more co-operatively, more compactly
PRODUCTION:		
• *Forms of ownership & management*	—private ownership of land—a collective resource—for speculation and profit	—management of land through community and regional land trusts
• *How resources get distributed*	—allocation of land for development by market forces, not to improve eco/social health	—uses to which land is put to be decided in accordance with ecological & social criteria
• *Technologies*	—technologies of transportation and production encourage centralization of economic activity & decentralization of settlement	—cultivation of "environmentally-friendly" technologies; consideration of total impacts

fight for social justice. Thirdly, only by participating in decision-making and learning how to trade short-term advantages off against long-term consequences will people develop the maturity to live in harmony with nature.

At present, people are encouraged to pursue their own private ends while leaving management of the "common good" to state officials. However, centralized institutions will not succeed in stabilizing humanity's relationship with nature. In addition to having a technocratic mandate, such institutions are limited by notions of the sacredness of private property and the right of individuals to speculate and become rich. A profound change must occur in the structure of people's thinking and values, and in the kind of aspirations they hold for themselves. To make peace with nature, society must emulate nature, at least in certain respects. It must become more self-regulating at the community level— learning to live in balance with regional ecosystems—rather than relying on government to impose "order" from above. However, if we don't opt for a democratic solution to the ecological crisis soon, authoritarian solutions, however unwieldy, will become more necessary and inevitable.

"...decentralizing and democratizing power relationships will not automatically "solve" the ecological crisis."

A second principle of ecological democracy is that humans must include, in their deliberations, a concern for the needs and interests of other members of the life-community. A third principle is that the difference between how the technocracy *talks* about democracy and how it *practices* it provides an opening to be taken advantage of. People living in a technocratic society are consistently denied the right to make the decisions which affect their lives and their immediate environments, and this is particularly obvious whenever some unpopular, ecologically damaging "development" project is proposed. But it should be pointed out that decentralizing and democratizing power relationships will not automatically "solve" the ecological crisis. There is nothing *inherent* in the democratizing process that guarantees conflicting interests will be harmonized, that humans will consider the needs of other species, or that they will be willing to sacrifice present "perks" for long-term sustainability.

Strategic Issues

A number of issues relate to the preconditions for achieving sustainability. The first has to do with the development of a radical consciousness on the part of the planetariat. Three things are needed: radical *values*, a radical *analysis*, and a radical *vision*. As I mentioned earlier, planetarian values are implicitly radical in that they resist and reject "development." However, without an analysis of technocratic institutions, and a vision of how society might be changed, planetarians tend to aim at piecemeal (and, ultimately, ineffectual) reforms. At least, this has been my experience in Ontario. The point of looking at society as a mode of reproduction is that it is not just a few "bad apple" politicians who are at fault, or a few bad laws, it is a whole *structure of values and institutions* which must be changed.

A second issue pertains to objective things that need to happen before social change will come about. So long as the economy "works," those who are challenging society's values and institutions will continue to remain relatively marginal and ineffective. Only when the system puts people's *economic* survival at risk will those who lack the planetariat's cultural and ecological perspective begin demanding more change.

When the system ceases to "deliver the goods," as it is beginning to do for many individuals currently employed in resource or pollution-intensive industries, it, in effect, violates the "social contract" that has kept many well-paid working people relatively loyal to the system. This creates an opportunity to build alliances between groups which have tended to be unsympathetic to one another, such as Natives, environmentalists, and workers in resource industries, such as the forest products industry.[3] No new mode of reproduction will ever come into being until new ways of making a living are found:

> People are aware of the social costs of the system, but it is a system that, after all, does deliver the goods along with the costs. In the absence of alternative systems that could deliver the goods without the costs, it is unthinkable to reject this one. Once such alternatives have been firmly established, it will be possible to give resistance and struggle a positive meaning for the many who suffer from the deprivations of the system, but see no way to change it.[4]

An alliance between workers and the planetariat gives the search for such institutions much greater force.

A big challenge for social change activists is learning how to balance working for immediate reforms with the need to maintain a long-term vision of radical social change. The positions that we take on this issue are related to our views of government.

As long as the state, at whatever level, is the agency that makes decisions about how land will be used, then local citizens' groups have no choice but to try to influence state policy. This is the *defensive* part of our struggle; it amounts to putting roadblocks in the path of development. This phase shades over into what might be called a *transitional* phase—proposing and fighting for reforms which help address immediate problems, but which have longer-term consequences, potentially constituting the building blocks of a new society. A third, *radical*, phase involves educating people about the link between our current mode of reproduction and the planetary crisis, and the need to build a new mode: a new way of relating to ourselves and to nature.

To juggle these different phases requires combining different ways of relating to government. Possible strategies include: attempting to get elected to state positions in order to use them to strengthen grassroots movements and push through needed reforms; developing so-called "co-production" schemes where citizens become directly involved in carrying out government functions (an example of this would be the new *Temagami Stewardship Council* involving members of the Teme-Augama Anishnabai and representatives of the Ontario provincial government— see Chapter 14), and reducing our dependence on the state and seeking to rebuild our community networks—networks which in the past did a lot of the things that we now expect government to do. I would argue that the planetarian movement needs to do all of these things simultaneously. Previously, Greens have found it difficult to avoid making one strategy (particularly, electoral activity) the be-all and end-all of their work.

Hopefully, as we make breakthroughs in fostering grassroots action for sustainability, we can reflect on the lessons and gain a better understanding of how to move towards a sustainable society.

Endnotes:

(1) See, for instance, Robyn Eckersley, "Green Politics and the New Class: Selfishness or Virtue?" *Political Studies* 37, no. 2 (1989): 205-223.

(2) Donald Worster, "Water and the Flow of Power," in *Man, Nature and Technology*, ed. by Erik Baark and Uno Svedin (London: Macmillan Press, 1988) 109, 121.

(3) Examples of where this is beginning to occur include Earth First! activist Judi Bari's work in California and Oregon, and the Tin-Wis Coalition being organized in British Columbia.

(4) C. George Benello and Dimitrios Rousopoulos, "Introduction," in *The Case for Participatory Democracy*, ed. by C. George Benello and Dimitrios Rousopoulos (New York: Grossman Publishers, 1971).

Reclaiming The Power Of Community

Priscilla Boucher

Our understanding of power has been shaped by the mechanistic worldview which sees power as an attribute of limited quantity which is distributed unevenly to isolated individuals. Power is something which someone or some group *has*. It is something which can be seized, taken, given, or "put in its place."

This static view of power emphasises the separation between those who "have" power (the power-full) and those who don't (the power-less). Because there is only so much power to go around, one can only have more power by taking it away from soneone else (a win-lose situation where their gain is another's loss), or by persuading those with power to give some of it up (in which case they continue to depend on the goodwill of the powerful who can always "take it back"). And of course those with more power are free to use it as they wish , constrained only by their own morality. Although we need to understand the workings of power in our society, analyses which focus solely on the ways in which the powerful exercise "power-over" others contribute to our own sense of powerlessness and victimization. It gives us the sense that domination is so total that resistance is futile.

A more dynamic understanding of power focusses on the connections between the individuals involved. Power, as a relation, *flows* from "sender" to "receiver." The effectiveness of the exercise of power by the "sender" depends on the degree to which the "receivers" consent to the relation. Orders, to be effective, must be obeyed. In this view, power is neither positive nor negative. The form it takes depends on the nature of the relationships through which it flows.

Starhawk in *Truth Or Dare: Encounters with Power, Authority and Mystery* (Harper & Row, 1990) distinguishes between three forms of power: power-over, power-with, and power-from-within. The exercise of "power-over" ranges from the overt use of force and violence to more subtle forms of persuasion. For "power-over" to flow effectively, there has to be some element of submissiveness, dependency, or fear on the part of the receivers of this power. In exchange for our obedience we get that which is not directly or easily available to us—we get that which we fear losing. In agreeing to this exchange we fail to realize that the powerful need what we agree to give them (our labor, resources, approval, etc.). Our consent is also obtained through mechanisms which persuade us through the manufacture of a "truth" which serves the powerful. This "truth" defines the ways in which we should "see" and "be" in the world. There are no alternatives. Other truths, other ways of seeing and being are over-shadowed, devalued and discredited. But the power to define, like all power, is a relation. It depends for its effectiveness on the existence of others who are willing to "believe" their truth. To accept this truth is to deny our own experiences, strengths and power.

"when the number of individuals who are prepared to exercise their power-from-within increases, *power-over* begins its conversion to *power-with."*

As individuals, we exercise "power-from-within" when we choose to act from our inner sense of integrity and "truth." The strength of "power-from-within" does not come from external authority nor from possession of the means of coercion. It emerges from within us. It comes from our willingness to act from, and to protect, the deep bonds that connect us with each other and with the Earth. It is "power-from-within" that gives us the strength to speak out and to join with others in withdrawing our consent for relations of "power-over." As receivers of "power-over," we have the option of refusing to act as a vehicle for the exercise of someone else's power. It is at the point of reception that we are presented with the opportunity of refusal—the exercise of our power-from-within. It is in our willingness and readiness to exercise this power that the authority of "power-over" is weakened. It is when the number of individuals who are prepared to exercise their power-from-within increases that "power-over" begins its conversion to "power-with."

In joining with others we exercise "power-with"—the collective side of "power-from-within." "Power-with" is "the power not to command, but to suggest and be listened to, to begin something and see it happen. The source of power-with is the willingness of others to listen to our ideas. We could call that willingness respect, not for a role, but for each unique person." This form of power is exercised within the limits of community—the net of relations which sanctions the ordered use of our individual and collective powers. It is a fluid, constructive and creative form of leadership which "retains its strength only through restraint. It affirms, shapes, and guides a collective decision—but it cannot enforce its will on the group or push it in a direction contrary to community desires." To do so would be to exert "power-over"—the form of power normally exercised within hierarchical positions of authority.

The linking of "power-from-within" and "power-with" offers us a clear alternative to the dominant form of "power-over." It is through the exercise of these powers that we recover our capacity to act, to resist, to create.

7

Our Home And Native Land? Creating An Eco-Constitution In Canada

Michael M'Gonigle

Since western industrial societies have evolved to the point where their impact on the natural world is ecologically disastrous, it follows that their continued, sustainable evolution must be based upon a wholly transformed way of perceiving the world and operating within it. If the 1990s are truly to be a "turn-around decade," then the very basis of the western world—its source of power—must be turned on its head. To do this means re-evaluating the relationships among politics, economics and the land, and tampering radically with the constitutional basis of modern democracies.

Michael M'Gonigle—Chairperson of Greenpeace Foundation, Canada, and Associate Professor in the School of Natural Resources Management at Simon Fraser University in Vancouver, B.C.—calls this process "eco-constitutionalism." Because of Canada's continuing constitutional instability, he regards the country as having a unique opportunity to enshrine community control in its legislative fabric, thereby perhaps blazing a trail that other nations must soon follow.

L ast summer, people across Canada quietly cheered as a lone Cree Indian, Elijah Harper, feather in hand, rose day after day in the Manitoba legislature, and said "No." A member of the House, Harper's acquiescence was essential if a national constitutional amendment, the so-called Meech Lake Accord, was to pass one of the two remaining provincial legislatures, and thus come into law across the country. Instead, with Elijah's eleventh hour veto, Canada's history took an unpredictable, but potentially very promising, turn.

The passage of time has intensified the constitutional conflict. Confrontations are getting frequent and hot between the federal government and native people across the country who seek land claims settlements. Meanwhile, the constitutional challenge has gained huge momentum throughout Québec. This turmoil has, however, thrust Canada into a unique position in the industrialized democratic world. Fundamental debate about the structure and future of the state is now the order-of-the day in Canada, whether one is a Québec separatist, a native lands claimant, a radical ecologist, or even just someone who simply reads the newspaper at night. Such a national re-examination is occurring nowhere else in the West.

In this vein, ecologists have, of course, long argued that we must "decentralize" society in order to survive. What this means for the structure of governance has, however, been little considered; a unifying vision of how a decentralist constitution might work is lacking. The constitutional crisis in Canada offers an unexpected historical opportunity for ecologists to put this situation right, if we can begin to develop here a new conception of the state and its constitution—an "eco-constitution"—and translate that vision into a broader social movement.

Yet even before we begin, we must grasp that to talk of community control or of an eco-constitution is, however, to challenge the direction of modern history. The advocates of Western-style liberal democracy, and the free market economics of globalization which accompany it, have achieved such success in recent decades that their vision has gained the status of an almost final truth. As a now famous article in *Fortune* magazine proclaimed last year, we are at "the end point of mankind's (sic) ideological evolution and the emergence of Western liberal democracy as the final form of human government."

In practice, this belief entails acceptance of an expansionist corporate agenda on a global scale, the antithesis of the ecologist's locally self-reliant, decentralist vision for the future.

In Canada, in 1988, for example, the federal government delivered the country into a subservient "free trade" deal with the United States, a legally binding arrangement which, in effect, declares illegal a vast array of economic and regulatory tools that might be used to protect the Canadian environment, its resource base, and its economy. Since that date, the Canadian government has systematically targeted for destruction the cultural institutions that give the country a distinct political identity, such as the national broadcasting, railroad, and medical care systems.

Thus, while we may speak of local control, *Economicus Americanus* is taking over Canada. While we talk of community sustainability, the opposite credo is actually driving political life throughout the world: external expansionism, not internal reform. The idea of the eco-constitution may provide a powerful alternative to the ideology of economic globalization, but it does so in an increasingly hostile environment.

The Fallacy Of The Liberal Constitution?

Like the state system itself, the Western concept of the "constitution" is but a few centuries old. Its ideological roots are the same as those of the market economy that grew up in tandem with the modern state—society as nothing more than an aggregation of competitive individuals.

This "liberal constitution" is designed primarily to regulate the political relations between the state and its individual citizens. Economic relations of the "free market" are on principle outside politics, an area where the state should not intrude. Similarly, the free individual, not the "community," is the focus for constitutional consideration. And, of course, the natural environment which surrounds and pervades the whole structure is simply not considered at all.

In contrast to this legalistic approach, the historical reality is that society is "self-constituted" by the workings of the whole—of economic forces acting on individuals, of central government on communities, of society on nature. Our legal constitution is, in contrast, confined to a small part of that whole, essentially to central political administration. But its assumptions are so powerful that, enshrining them into that new creature called the "state" has dramatically shaped the evolution of Western society over the past three or four centuries.

In the Western world, sovereignty, *by definition*, emanates from the top. Politically, our national constitutions simply assume that power is to be centralized, and then they seek to "balance" centralized powers by keeping them apart. This is the implication of the famous "separation of powers" between the executive, legislative and judicial branches of government, all top-down centralized institutions. Whether or not there is a need for limits on centralized power itself is not asked.

Even in federal states such as Canada, formal political power is concentrated in a few capitals, subject only to periodic general elections. The nature of the Meech Lake Accord (a product of secret negotiations involving 11 men: the prime minister and 10 premiers) exemplifies the structural dominance of a very centralized, male hierarchy. In this light, that it was toppled by a Native leader, Elijah Harper, in a provincial legislature, is not without significance.

The signal achievement of the liberal constitution is to confer political rights on individuals within this structure of centralized power. Our constitutions do not, however, confer such rights on geographical community, let alone ask the question of how much social power should remain there. Instead, protecting community interests becomes delegitimized. Those who oppose a toxic disposal site in their valley are dismissed for demonstrating a selfish NIMBY (Not In My Back Yard) syndrome. Yet to isolate the individual as the ultimate social actor is clearly incorrect—after all, the community was there first, and individuals are born into, and molded by, it.

In short, our constitution is founded on several false assumptions about central power, the nature of the individual, and the irrelevance of the community. Our constitutional premises are false on another important fundamental as well—the belief that the competitive market is an objective mechanism where politics has no role, where the market can be "free." In fact, however, the competitive market mechanism is not merely a tool but has its own internal constitution; for example, its inherent tendencies to grow and expand, and to increase its levels of resource throughput and consumption.

"Any constitutional debate which takes ecological and cultural sustainability seriously must begin by tossing out the liberal conception of the constitution itself."

These limitations have had profound consequences for how modern society has evolved, and they continue to limit future possibilities. Simply put, with communities and the natural environment politically unrepresented, and with individuals fragmented into little social atoms, the expansionist tendencies of the economic constitution have successfully overcome myriad local resistances to become the driving force of Western history.

Ultimately the purpose of any constitution, however defined, is to constitute the social collective over time. Despite its philosophical deference to individual autonomy and free markets, to democratic government and bureaucratic accountability, the liberal constitution has helped constitute us as the opposite of its earliest premises—as a centralized mass society, devoid of distinctive individualism and community, dominated by overgrown economic and bureaucratic hierarchies.

Any constitutional debate which takes ecological and cultural sustainability seriously must begin by tossing out the liberal conception of the constitution itself. As Québecers realize, we are engaged in a collective process of "social self-constitution", of defining how we actually *evolve as a culture.* The western constitution, as presently conceived, is simply not up to this task. Indeed, by setting economic power free to pursue its own ends, the real result of the liberal constitution is to create society itself *as a mere side-effect* of the pursuit of economic growth and power. We are, in sum, a product of both a "formal" constitution (the legal rules of state) and—especially—of an "informal" constitution (the operational rules of the competitive market).

The Canadian experience is exemplary. Libraries overflow with the works of political economists who have demonstrated how Canada's role as a raw resource exporter into the international market has shaped the economic, political and cultural fabric of the country. Descriptions of our economy in centralist geographical terms like "core and periphery," or in hierarchical economic terms like "hegemony" and "domination," abound in the literature.

Take, for example, my home, British Columbia. Forestry is the Number One industry, and calls the shots with the provincial government. Short-term governmental policy is dictated by the fear of job loss in an industry which is already overcutting and "shedding" labor to remain internationally competitive. The inability to implement sustainable long-term alternatives, like community forestry, is dictated by the informal constitution—all the forest land is "owned" by a handful of multinational forest giants. Their 25-year "tenure" rights give them *de facto* control over virtually the whole forest land base of the province. In theory, tenure could be allocated to anyone; in practice, it has been contractually locked up by international corporations. Options which might create meaningful local control and allow for sustainable forestry are met with cries of "Private property! Expropriation!" Politically, they inspire fears of capital flight, economic collapse, and social chaos.

"Power does not get put, nor stay, in its place without a bigger power behind it."

Thus does the informal, corporate constitution dominate the informal, governmental one, and shape our future self-constitution. And where is democratic politics in all this? In a public with so little effect that it must erupt in continuous protest to be heard. Though in theory rooted in democracy, the very legitimacy of the environmental protest is questioned, and labelled disparagingly as "single interest groups," "protesters," "preservationists." Similarly, native opponents whose millenia-old community land base is destroyed for a quick return on investment are forced to the barricades and criminalized. Meanwhile, every year, the rate of cut goes up.

Political ecologists are *especially* aware of the fatal failures of centralization and thus envision the radical decentralization of the state, of pulling power back down to the community. But so, too, free-traders seek to humble states where national borders provide a barrier to the free flow of capital or, worse, a forum for citizens to assert democratic interests over those of the corporation. This, for example, is the *de facto* constitutional function of GATT (the General Agreement on Tariffs and Trade), to limit state freedom by putting whole areas of economic management politically off limits.

In this situtation, those who seek progressive change must be ever mindful. In developing an eco-constitution, the organizing foundation is the community; but the vehicle to achieve that must be the reassertion of political decision over economic power—of the formal over the informal constitution. In the shadow of *Economicus Americanus*, if civic society is to be recovered, and social interests to prevail, the state must be transformed; it must not just wither away.

The Promise Of The Eco-constitution

When a nation-state's constitution is questioned, everything is opened up, everything becomes possible. However, the real object of concern is not the state alone, but the structure of centralized society as a whole. If the territorial community is to become a central organizing concept of society, there will need to be political power of some sort to allow it to happen in the first place, and to protect it later on as well. Power does not get put, nor stay, in its place without a bigger power behind it.

A fundamental fallacy of Western history is the belief that power does, and more importantly should, reside at the top—in parliaments and cathedrals, in the corporate boardroom, in the Crown—rather than in the bottom, in the people in their geographical places. In contrast, the essence of the eco-constitution is to root social power in territorial community. Institutions grow out of those roots and, in the end, survive by keeping them strong and by themselves not growing too tall. If we grow too tall and proud, we will crash. To maintain stability, power must be delegated, not from the Crown down, but from the community up.

In the quest for the eco-constitution, native people are key. In Canada, across the land, their history, their so-called myths, and their elders tell us how it is to do that which we must now all do on this one planet—learn to live in place. This is not just romantic philosophy but has practical significance. For example, Native people are the clearest articulators of the foundation of the eco-constitution—their claim to "title" to their ancestral lands. In making this claim, they deny that sovereignty emanates from the legislative buildings in Victoria, the Parliament in Ottawa, or from the Queen at Westminister. It emanates from the land itself, and is expressed through their community on that land.

"The essence of the eco-constitution is to root social power in territorial community. ...To maintain stability, power must be delegated, not from the Crown down, but from the community up."

Let me put all this another way. In the west, we set out no ultimate justificiation for the power of government, other than that history has made it so. The Queen does not rule by divine decree, but by accident of birth; neither does Parliament turn to religious texts to justify its existence. It is there by historical accident. But the Crown, through its ministers, has an historical monopoly on the use of legitimate force. It has sovereignty, and that is enough to justify its position. This is the perspective of so-called "positive law."

In contrast, native cultures tell us that human laws must reflect natural laws, that there is a larger order to which human society must conform, and that one understands that embedded order by participating in it where it is. To recognize that modernity has lost contact with the experience both of nature, and of a level of community which works with nature, is not something to toss off lightly. It has left us vulnerable and dependent.

Even today, we do not deny the existence of some reference point for our affairs, but that truth is found not in the laws of nature but in those of economics. In the lush coastal rainforest of Clayoquot Sound on Canada's west coast, local communities are trying to stop clearcut logging, to save some of the natural forest and varied habitat, to preserve a fragment of the original biological diversity for the next millenium. That demand is challenged because it threatens jobs, and is dismissed as "preservationism." In contrast, when the major logging company in the area closes its sawmill and throws 300 employees out of work because of "international market conditions," that act is accepted with inevitability. No blame is attached.

Toward A Canadian Eco-Constitution

To talk of natural law is radical, because it means that we are accountable. We cannot simply proceed regardless of the consequences, but must develop both a larger understanding of how we constitute ourselves as a collective consciousness, and a reorganized structure for doing so.

Today, all levels of government are enmeshed in the homogenizing pressures and aggressive institutions of the informal market constitution. All our leaders, whatever their stand on national unity vs. provincial rights, are old school economic thinkers, committed to the corporate vision of growth and free market expansionism. Formally, the political authority of local governments—whether municipalities, regional districts or counties—is delegated down from the provinces; informally, the choices facing these levels are dictated by the centralized economy. A rational urban transportation system?   Check with General Motors. Recycling? Ask the packaging industry. Energy conservation? No thank you; Québec Hydro would rather flood out the Cree.

Québec's approach to independence reflects this situation. While it seeks to protect its "cultural autonomy" by political realignments, its premier is going hell bent in the other direction economically, basing the Québecois economy of the future on North America's grandest and most destructive economic mega-project, the flooding of a vast proportion of Québec's wildlands behind hydro-electric dams at James Bay, to provide electricity for export to the United States. This is very old-fashioned planning, especially in light of the clear lessons of the "soft" energy revolution. But it maintains the old structures just a little bit longer.

In Canada, the key to changing all this is a *local veto* in a new *third level* of government. In the eco-constitution, this level would everywhere be recognized as the ultimate source of sovereignty (in native parlance, "title"), with *limited* jurisdictional authority *delegated up* to other levels. This would transform the role of provinces because natural resources (that is, the whole land base) are today owned by the Crown in right of the province. This is the source of so much of Canada's economic wealth—from the forests and mines, to hydro-electricity and water. Who controls it, and for what purpose, are key questions.

Under the prevailing constitutional approach, Québec's separation from Canada would lead to an accelerated attack on the province's resource base—traditionally regarded as "peripheral" by economists— and on the native communities who live there. Counterbalancing federal jurisdiction over the environment and native rights would be lost. In contrast, if the local native nations who presently live there had a political veto over such developments, an eco-constitution would not only shift political decision-making but, even more importantly, it could begin a fundamental economic re-orientation as well. Thus would the eco-constitution merge the informal into the formal constitution.

From this perspective, new approaches emerge on a range of specifics. If we wish to encourage local economies and local sustainability, should there still be a single money system? If rural areas are not to continue subsidizing urban ones, should resource rents from the sale of "Crown" forests and minerals perhaps stay at the local level, rather than going into provincial coffers? If the interests of place are truly to be protected, how large should the territorial unit of third level government be? What would be the role and powers of higher levels of government?

There are no final answers to such questions because, for one thing, they simply have not been considered. It is time in Canada to begin working them out through political debate. Despite the fears which such a grand re-design will instill, in reality such political restructuring would lead to greater efficiencies in numerous areas of economic life. For example, if the Québec Cree, or the small towns of rural B.C., could block hydro projects on their rivers, Montreal and Vancouver would simply have to do what the experts have long been telling us—become more efficient, conserve, reduce demand not increase supply, and recycle. Whether it is energy, agriculture, or health that is at issue, a third-level veto would inherently tend to move toward internal social reform at the core, not further expansionism at the periphery.

"By having progressive jurisdictional powers held within a coordinating confederation, the eco-constitution would build in a "double veto"—the local community restraining economic exploitation by outside interests, the confederal authority constraining local abuse."

Contrary to our social evolution since the "free market" broke loose from its communal bonds a few centuries ago, eco-constitutionalism re-asserts the primacy of political, over economic, decisions. Re-embedding the economy within the community turns our economically-driven modern history on its head; the eco-constitution is the foundation for the transformative economy, not the reverse. Here the state is important, for one thing, as the contemporary source of democratic legitimacy, of politics itself.

In Canada, many continuing roles would exist for a confederal authority. Equitable relations between third-level communities must be maintained within some overall "confederation," and the common interests of this confederation represented in some fashion. Protection of the communitarian base from external aggression, including regulation of inter-community trade (at various levels) to protect the community economy, would also be necessary. This is exactly the opposite of the surrender of authority under the Canada-U.S. Free Trade Agreement, or the GATT rules. Maintenance of "national standards" in areas such as human and democractic rights, environmental protection, protection of minorities, and social welfare could also be within the limited jurisdiction of some confederal authority, or a transformed Charter of Rights *and Obligations.*

By having progressive jurisdictional powers held within a coordinating confederation, the eco-constitution would build in a "double veto"— the local community with the authority to control exploitation by outside interests, the confederal authority constraining local abuse. Over the past several hundred years, the absence of a local veto combined with the inherently expansionist tendency of central power to exploit (rather than to protect) local territories has lead us to the brink of ecological, and cultural, collapse. By creating a double veto, an eco-constitution would turn this around, tending to seek a higher, rather than a lower, common denominator.

Social Movements For A Social Constitution

With the unique historical opportunity now facing Canada, the collective voices of social movements are essential ones in the evolving constitutional debate. Natives, ecologists, progressive Québecois nationalists, feminists, radical labor, the "alternatives" movement, provide the core constituency. But a successful eco-constitutional movement would need to become a broader movement based on a larger "social" liberalism where collective values are achieved, not by ameliorative, trickle-down social programs, but by a transformative institutional redesign. We will be different in the years ahead; our "social self-constitution" will evolve us into something unrecognizably different from today. But we could become so gradually, by creating a new dynamic for political, and economic, power.

With unconstrained corporate power running amok on the planet, we find ourselves confronting a choice between seeking a new consciousness and constitution, and awaiting an inevitable catastrophe. In Canada, by prying open the western constitutional model that has so unconsciously reduced our social prospects, Elijah Harper and Québec nationalists may just help Canadians to recognize, and deal with, that choice.

8

The Meaning
Of Confederalism

Murray Bookchin

The evolution of western society toward more urban and centralized forms of organization has not occurred arbitrarily nor in a vaccuum. The cultural stagnation, authoritarianism and parochialism characteristic of many rural communities has been the motive force for many peoples' exodus from the countryside. This points to the fact that decentralization, localism and self-sufficiency, although worthy ideals, are not in and of themselves sufficent to make up the new society that many people are currently striving for.

Equally important in the decentralist vision are true democracy, community and confederalism, as Murray Bookchin—the widely-read promoter of "social ecology"—here describes.

Few arguments have been used more effectively to challenge the case for face-to-face participatory democracy than the claim that we live in a "complex society." Modern population centers, we are told, are too large and too concentrated to allow for direct decision-making at a grassroots level. And our economy is too "global," presumably, to unravel the intricacies of production and commerce. In our present transnational, often highly centralized social system, it is better to enhance representation in the state, to increase the efficiency of bureaucratic institutions, we are advised, than to advance utopian "localist" schemes of popular control over political and economic life.

After all, such arguments often run, centralists are all really "localists" in the sense that they believe in "more power to the people"—or at least, to their representatives. And surely a good representative is always eager to know the wishes of his or her "constituents" (to use another of those arrogant substitutes for "citizens").

But face-to-face democracy? Forget the dream that in our "complex" modern world we can have any democratic alternative to the nation-state! Many pragmatic people, including socialists, often dismiss arguments for that kind of "localism" as otherworldly—with good-natured condescension at best and outright derision at worst. Indeed, some years back, I was challenged to explain how my decentralist views would prevent, say, Troy, New York, from dumping its untreated wastes into the Hudson River, from which downstream cities like Perth Amboy draw their drinking water.

On the surface of things, arguments like this for centralized government seem rather compelling. A structure that is "democratic," to be sure, but still largely top-down is assumed as necessary to prevent one locality from afflicting another ecologically. But conventional economic and political arguments against decentralization, ranging from the fate of Perth Amboy's drinking water to our alleged "addiction" to petroleum, rest on a number of very problematical assumptions. Most disturbingly, they rest on an unconscious acceptance of the economic status quo.

Decentralism And Self-Sustainability

The assumption that what currently exists must necessarily exist is the acid that corrodes all visionary thinking. Must the present-day extravagant international division of labor necessarily exist in order to satisfy human needs? Or has it been created to provide extravagant profits for multinational corporations? Are we to ignore the ecological consequences of plundering the Third World of its resources, insanely interlocking modern economic life with petroleum-rich areas whose ultimate products include air pollutants and petroleum-derived carcinogens? To ignore the fact that our "global economy" is the result of burgeoning industrial bureaucracies and a competitive grow-or-die market economy is incredibly myopic.

There are sound ecological reasons for achieving a certain measure of self-sustainability. A massive national and international division of labor is extremly wasteful in the literal sense of that term. Not only does an excessive division of labor make for over-organization in the form of huge bureaucracies and tremendous expenditures of resources in transporting materials over great distances, it reduces the possibilities of effectively recycling wastes, avoiding pollution that may have its source in highly concentrated industrial and population centers, and making sound use of local or regional raw materials.

On the other hand, we cannot ignore the fact that relatively self-sustaining communities in which crafts, agriculture, and industries serve definable networks of confederally organized communities enrich the opportunities and stimuli to which individuals are exposed and make for more rounded personalities with a rich sense of selfhood and competence. The Greek ideal of the rounded citizen in a rounded environment—one that reappeared in Charles Fourier's utopian works—was long cherished by the anarchists and socialists of the last century.

"Decentralism, a face-to-face participatory democracy, and a localist emphasis on community values should be viewed as all of one piece."

We should not, I believe, lose sight of what it means to live an ecological way of life, not merely follow sound ecological practices. The multitude of handbooks that teach us how to conserve, invest, eat, and buy in an "ecologically responsible" manner are a travesty of the more basic need to reflect on what it means to think—yes, to reason—and to live ecologically in the full meaning of the term. Thus, I would hold that to garden organically is more than a good form of husbandry and a good source of nutrients; it is above all a way to place oneself directly in the food web by personally cultivating the very substances one consumes to live, and by returning to one's environment what one elicits from it. Food thus becomes more than a form of material nutriment. The soil one tills, the living things one cultivates and consumes, the compost one prepares—all unite in an ecological continuum to feed the spirit as well as the body, sharpening one's sensitivity to the nonhuman and human world around us. Such monumental changes as the dissolution of the nation state and its substitution with a participatory democracy, then, do not occur in a psychological vacuum where the political structure alone is changed. In the case of Perth Amboy's drinking water, I argued that in a society that was radically veering toward decentralist, participatory democracy, guided by communitarian and ecological principles, it is only reasonable to suppose that people would not choose such an irresponsible social dispensation as would allow the waters of the Hudson to be so polluted. Decentralism, a face-to-face participatory democracy, and a localist emphasis on community values should be viewed as all of one piece. This "one piece" involves not only a new politics but a new political culture that embraces new ways of thinking and feeling, and new human interrelationships, including the ways we experience the natural world. Words like "politics" and "citizenship" would be redefined by the rich meanings they acquired in the past, and enlarged for the present.

It is not very difficult to show—item by item—how the international division of labor can be greatly attenuated by using local and regional resources, implementing ecotechnologies, rescaling human consumption along rational (indeed, healthful) lines, and emphasizing quality production that provides lasting (instead of throwaway) means of life. There is a need, too, for regional integration and to interlink resources among ecocommunities. For decentralized communities are inevitably interdependent upon one another.

Problems Of Decentralism

Without such wholistic cultural and political changes, notions of decentralism that emphasize localist isolation and a degree of self-sufficiency may lead to cultural parochialism and chauvinism. Parochialism can lead to problems that are as serious as a "global" mentality that overlooks the uniqueness of cultures, the peculiarities of ecosystems and ecoregions, and the need for a humanly-scaled community life that makes a participatory democracy possible. We must find a way of sharing the world with other humans and with nonhuman forms of life, a view that is often difficult to attain in overly "self-sufficient" communities.

The concepts of local self-reliance and self-sustainability can be highly misleading. I can certainly agree with David Morris of the Institute for Local Self-Reliance, for example, that if a community can produce the things it needs, it should probably do so. But self-sustaining communities cannot produce *all* the things they need—unless it involves a return to a back-breaking way of village life that historically often prematurely aged its men and women with hard work and allowed them very little time for political life beyond the immediate confines of the community itself.

"It is a troubling fact that neither decentralization nor self-sufficiency in itself is necessarily democratic ...small is not necessarily beautiful."

Today we can produce the basic means of life—and a good deal more—in an ecological society that is focused on the production of high-quality useful goods. This is not the same as advocating a kind of "collective" capitalism, in which one community functions like a single entrepreneur, with a sense of proprietorship toward its resources. Such a system of cooperatives once again marks the beginnings of a market system of distribution, as cooperatives become entangled in the web of "bourgeois rights"—that is, in contracts and bookkeeping that focus on the exact amounts a community will receive in "exchange" for what it delivers to others. This deterioration occurred among some of the worker-controlled enterprises that functioned like capitalistic enterprises in Barcelona after the workers expropriated them in the Spanish Revolution in 1936.

It is a troubling fact that neither decentralization nor self-sufficiency in itself is necessarily democratic. Plato's ideal city in the *Republic* was indeed designed to be self-sufficient, but its self-sufficiency was meant to maintain a warrior as well as a philosophical élite. Indeed, its capacity to preserve its self-sufficiency depended upon its ability, like Sparta, to resist the seemingly "corruptive" influence of outside cultures (a characteristic, I may say, that still appears in many closed societies in the East).

Similarly, decentralization in itself provides no assurance that we will have an ecological society. A decentralized society can easily coexist with extremely rigid hierarchies. A striking example is European and Oriental feudalism, a social order in which princely, ducal, and baronial hierarchies were based on highly decentralized communities. With all due respect to Fritz Schumacher, small is not necessarily beautiful.

Nor does it follow that humanly-scaled communities and "appropriate technologies" in themselves constitute guarantees against domineering societies. In fact, for centuries humanity lived in villages and small towns, often with tightly organized social ties and even communistic forms of property. But these provided the material basis for highly despotic imperial states. What these self-sufficient, decentralized communities feared almost as much as the armies that ravaged them were the imperial tax-gatherers that plundered them.

Decentralization, localism, self-sufficiency, and even confederation— each taken singly—do not constitute a guarantee that we will achieve a rational, ecological society. In fact, all of them have at one time or another supported parochial communities, oligarchies, and even despotic regimes. To be sure, without the institutional structures that cluster around our use of these terms and without taking them in combination with each other, we cannot hope to achieve a free, ecologically oriented society.

Confederalism And Interdependence

What often leads to serious misunderstandings among decentralists is their failure in all too many cases to see the need for libertarian forms of confederation—which at least tends to counteract the tendency of decentralized communities to drift toward exclusivity and parochialism.

Confederalism is, above all, a network of administrative councils whose members or delegates are elected from popular face-to-face democratic assemblies in the various villages, towns, and even neighborhoods of large cities. The members of these confederal councils are strictly mandated, recallable, and responsible to the assemblies that choose them for the purpose of coordinating and administering the policies formulated by the assemblies themselves. Their function is thus a purely administrative and practical one, not a policy-making one like the function of representatives in republican systems of government.

A confederalist view involves a clear distinction between policy-making and the coordination and execution of adopted policies. Policy-making is exclusively the right of popular community assemblies based on the practices of participatory democracy. Administration and coordination are the responsibility of confederal councils, which become the means for interlinking villages, towns, neighborhoods, and cities into confederal networks. Power thus flows from the bottom up instead of from the top down and, in confederations, the flow of power from the bottom up diminishes with the scope of the federal council, ranging territorially from localities to regions, and from regions to ever-broader territorial areas.

"A confederalist view involves a clear distinction between policy-making and the coordination and execution of adopted policies. Policy-making is exclusively the right of popular community assemblies based on the practices of participatory democracy."

A crucial element in giving reality to confederalism is the interdependence of communities for an authentic mutualism based on shared resources, produce, and policy-making. If one community is not obliged to count on another or others generally to satisfy important material needs and realize common political goals in such a way that it is interlinked to a greater whole, exclusivity and parochialism are genuine possibilities.

Confederalism is thus a way of perpetuating the interdependence that should exist among communities and regions—indeed, it is a way of democratizing that interdependence without surrendering the principle of local control. While a reasonable measure of self-sufficiency is desirable for every locality and region, confederalism is a means of avoiding local parochialism on the one hand and an extravagant national and global division of labor on the other. In short, it is a way in which a community can retain its identity and roundedness while participating in a sharing way with the larger whole that makes up a balanced ecological society. Confederalism as a principle of social organization reaches its fullest development when the economy itself is confederalized by placing local farms, factories, and other needed enterprises in local municipal hands—that is, when a community, however large or small, begins to manage its own economic resources in an interlinked network with other communities. I would like to think that a confederal ecological society would be a sharing one, one based on the pleasure that is felt in distributing among communities according to their needs, not one in which "cooperative" capitalistic communities mire themselves in the *quid pro quo* of exchange relationships.

Confederation is thus the ensemble of decentralization, localism, self-sufficiency, interdependence—and more. This "more" is the indispensible moral education and character-building—what the Greeks called *paideia*—that makes for rational, active citizenship in a participatory democracy, unlike the passive constituents and consumers that we have today. In the end, there is no substitute for a conscious reconstruction of our relationship to each other and the natural world.

Confederalism, in effect, must be conceived as a whole: a consciously formed body of interdependencies that unites participatory democracy in municipalities with a scrupulously supervised system of coordination. It involves the dialectical development of independence and dependence into a more richly articulated form of interdependence. Confederalism is thus a fluid and ever-developing kind of social metabolism in which the identity of an ecological society is preserved through its differences and by virtue of its potential for ever greater differentiation. It is the point of departure for a new ecosocial history marked by a participatory evolution within society, and between society and the natural world.

Confederation As Dual Power

Confederalism is a vibrant tradition in the affairs of humanity, one that has a centuries-long history behind it. Confederations for generations tried to countervail a historical tendency nearly as old toward centralization and the creation of the nation-state.

If confederalism and statism are not seen as being in tension with each other—a tension in which the nation-state has used a variety of intermediaries like provincial goverments in Canada and state governments in the United States to create the illusion of "local control"—then the concept of confederation loses all meaning. Provincial autonomy in Canada and states' rights in the United States are no more confederal than "soviets" or councils were the medium for popular control that existed in tension with Stalin's totalitarian state.

This same concept of wholeness that applies to the interdependencies between municipalities also applies to the muncipality itself. The municipality is the most immediate political arena of the individual, the world that is literally a doorstep beyond the privacy of the family and the intimacy of personal friendships. In that primary political arena, where politics should be conceived in the Hellenic sense of literally managing the *polis* or community, the individual can be transformed from a mere person into an active citizen, from a private being into a public being. Given this crucial arena that literally renders the citizen a functional being who can participate directly in the future of society, we are dealing with a level of human interaction that is more basic (apart from the family itself) than any level that is expressed in representative forms of governance, where collective power is literally transmuted into power embodied by one or a few individuals. The municipality is thus the most authentic arena of public life, however much it may have been distorted over the course of history.

Unquestionably, there are now cities that are so large that they verge on being quasi-republics in their own right. In such cases, a minimal program might demand that confederations be established within the urban area—namely, among neighborhoods or definable districts—not only among the urban areas themselves. In a very real sense, these highly populated, sprawling, and oversized entities must ultimately be broken down institutionally into authentic muncipalities that are scaled to human dimensions and that lend themselves to participatory democracy.

Where city councils and mayoral offices in large cities provide an arena for battling the concentration of power in an increasingly strong state or provincial executive and, even worse, in regional jurisdictions that may cut across many such cities (Los Angeles is a notable example), to run candidates for the city council may be the only recourse we have, in fact, for arresting the development of increasingly authoritarian state institutions and helping to restore an institutionally decentralized democracy.

It will no doubt take a long time to *physically* decentralize an urban entity such as New York City into authentic municipalities and ultimately into communes. But there is no reason why an urban entity of such a huge magnitude cannot be slowly decentralized *institutionally*. Libertarian municipalists must always keep the distinction between institutional and physical decentralization clearly in mind, and recognize that the former is entirely achievable even while the latter may take years to attain.

Draft Of A Constitutional Declaration Of Local Sovereignty

Tom Reveille

When in the course of human events, it becomes necessary for citizens of a nation state to separate their nation from the state that threatens to destroy it, and to break bonds of allegiance to a government allegedly of their own making but actually foreign to their vital interests and security, both solidarity and conscience require that they explore the necessity of their action.

We hold these truths to be self-evident: that Life—and Freedom, Her other self—are the supreme good; that only those laws that defend Life and Freedom demand our unquestioning obedience; that our sweet, uncomplaining Earth is, to the utmost of our knowledge, the Mother of all Life; and that in our time the very fabric of this wondrous adventure of Life, or Nature, is being torn asunder, so that there is great and increasing cause to fear the extinction of all consciousness by the end of this century.

Cancer stalks the Earth. Its name is profit, its nature poison. In the name of profit our lakes and rivers die. Our oceans are dying. Our freshwater aquifers are exhausted or contaminated. For the sake of profit our food, water and air are poisoned. Dwindling populations of fish gasp in our polluted streams. Birds fall from the air. The tribes of Life gutter and go out. Our children are poisoned in the womb or blasted in the cradle and precede their parents to the grave....

World-wide the plague is gaining momentum. In the face of a menace unprecedented in human history, where is our government—those we have charged in our *Constitution* with the protection of our life, liberty and well-being...? Incredibly, they are arrayed with the legions of profit against us. All efforts to defend ourselves within the bounds prescribed by our democratic traditions are countered by the overwhelming force of government in league with profit. Legislation is passed by profit not people, to protect not people but profit. Such legislation is forced and enforced upon us, devouring life, health and liberty....

The history of the present government of the United States is a history of

repeated injuries and usurpations all having as their direct object the establishment of an absolute tyranny over a free and sovereign people. In [NAME OF
COMMUNITY], these are some of the crimes perpetrated against us by this
government and its true beneficiaries:

[LIST OF GRIEVANCES SPECIFIC TO THE COMMUNITY OR GROUP
MAKING THIS DECLARATION]

Inasmuch as "to secure these rights governments are instituted among Men
[sic], deriving their just powers from the consent of the governed," any government destructive of life, health, liberty and property is clearly at war with its
people—both directly through its agencies, and indirectly by legitimizing and
protecting an economic system that permits, encourages, in many ways indeed
necessitates, devastation of our Home....

We who have borne for decades the assaults of the imperial corporate
government of the United States, who have endured its grievous and manifold
violations of our *Constitution*, can no longer sustain the pretense of a representative republic deriving its just powers from our consent. From a government
that betrays us to the genocidal, ecocidal, suicidal greed of the profiteers—and
is, indeed, chief among them—our allegiance is irrevocably withdrawn.

WE, THEREFORE, citizens of [COMMUNITY] do hereby dissolve all bonds of
allegiance and obedience to the evil empire destroying us and all our relations
and the Planet itself. We declare all nominal legislation not pursuant to our *Constitution* to be null and void and of no force—color of law merely and no law at
all. And we claim the inalienable right to be masters in our own home and to
exist—insofar as we are able—as a separate enclave of sanity amid the mur-
derous sociopathology of capitalism.

Within the boundaries of [COMMUNITY], the laws that govern our lives shall
henceforth be made constitutionally by a majority of the inhabitants thereof or
by our duly elected representatives. Within these boundaries no higher
authority shall be acknowledged.

Out of fear, mistaking the traditional trappings of democracy for the sub-
stance, we have blindly, foolishly trusted what we supposed was our constitutional government long after it had proved itself to be no such thing. No more.
Henceforth, under the *Constitution of the United States of America*, we shall
have trust only in ourselves and each other to defend our rights as free people,
to defend our lives and the Life of the Earth....

How this declaration will work out in practice and be given form in the coming days and months we have no way of knowing. But the principle of local self-
determination is not negotiable. In support of which, We the People of
[COMMUNITY] pledge to each other, to our Mother Earth, to our posterity, all that
we have—all that we are.

Part Three

Power In Place:
Community Control In Action

Nothing speaks as eloquently as example. What is most striking about the examples of community control presented here is that rarely, if ever, are they success stories about particular individuals. Almost always, local power is gained by collectives—organizations of people willing to do the daily, often tedious, work that it takes to actually get something accomplished. Someone once said, if you're looking for leadership, check out the reflection in the mirror. In other words, self-government in action is about ordinary people taking care of the whole. No heroes, no deferring of power to others who can do the job. The following essays and stories are offered as inspiration for those wishing to create community control!

9

Land Of The Free, Home Of The Brave: Iroquois Democracy

Oren Lyons

The decentralist call is a cry for freedom, for genuine community-based democracy. It is doubly ironic that this call should be articulated here on the continent of Turtle Island. First, because the United States of America was founded in reaction to the aristocracy and élite mercantilism of Europe—precisely as an attempt to fashion a new and democratic ideal. And, second, because this attempt by the newcomers to the continent was inspired by, and modelled upon, the form of government used among the original inhabitants—the Iroquois people, or Haudenosaunee—despite this history rarely being acknowledged.

The fact that the Haudenosaunee managed to create an enlightened and progressive form of democratic government is particularly interesting because, in their story, it emerged from a dark time of widespread violence and chaos—perhaps akin to that which we face today. The Honorable Oren Lyons, speaker for the Onondaga Nation, presented the following statement before a U.S. Senate Committee on Indian Affairs hearing (on Senate Resolution S. Con. 76) in 1987 to recognize the Iroquois origins of the U.S. Constitution. It stands as a timeless inspiration for our collective, democratic, future.

Early history, prior to the coming of the white man to this continent, receives little attention in the history books. But it was in these early times that the development of democratic processes came about on this land.

Upon the continent of North America, prior to the landfall of the white man, a great league of peace was formed, the inspiration of a prophet called the Peacemaker. He was a spiritual being, fulfilling the mission of organizing warring nations into a confederation under the Great Law of Peace. The principles of the law are peace, equity, justice, and the power of the good minds.

With the help and support of a like-minded man called Aionwatha, whom some people now call Hiawatha, an Onondaga by birth and a Mohawk by adoption, he set about the great work of establishing a union of peace under the immutable natural laws of the universe. He came to our Iroquois lands in our darkest hour, when the good message of how to live had been cast aside and naked power ruled, fueled by vengeance and blood lust. A great war of attrition engulfed the lands, and women and children cowered in fear of their own men. The leaders were fierce and merciless. They were fighting in a blind rage. Nations, homes, and families were destroyed, and the people were scattered. It was a dismal world of dark disasters where there seemed to be no hope. It was a raging proof of what inhumanity man is capable of when the laws and principles of life are thrown away.

The Peacemaker came to our lands, bringing the message of peace, supported by Aionwatha. He began the great work of healing the twisted minds of men. This is a long history, too long to recount here. Suffice it to say it is a great epic that culminated on the shores of the lake now called Onondaga where, after many years of hard work—some say perhaps even 100 years—he gathered the leaders, who had now become transformed into rational human beings, into a Grand Council, and he began the instructions of how the Great Law of Peace would work.

"The Peacemaker established the process of raising leaders for governance... and his authority is derived from the people..."

The Peacemaker set up the families into clans, and then he set up the leaders of the clans. He established that the League of Peace would be matriarchal and that each clan would have a clanmother. Thus, he established in law the equal rights of women.

He raised the leaders of each clan—two men, one the principal leader and the second his partner. They worked together for the good of the people. He called these two men *royane*, or the good minds, the peacemakers, and they were to represent the clans in council. Thus, he established the principles of representation of people in government.

Henceforth, he said, these men will be chosen by the clanmother, freely using her insight and wisdom. Her choice must first be ratified by the consensus of the clan. If they agree, then her choice must be ratified by full consensus of the Chiefs' Council of their nation. Then her choice must be ratified and given over to the Council of Chiefs who then call the Grand Council of the Great League of Peace, and they will gather at the nation that is raising the leader, and they would work together in ceremony.

He made two houses in each nation. One he called the Long House and the other he called the Mud House. They would work together in ceremony and council establishing the inner source of vitality and dynamics necessary for community.

He made two houses in the Grand Council, one called the Younger Brothers, consisting of the Oneida and the Cayuga Nations and later enlarging to include the Tuscarora. The other was the Elder Brothers, consisting of the Mohawks with the title Keepers of the Eastern Door, the Onondaga, whom he made the Firekeepers, and the Senecas, who were the Keepers of the Western Door. Now, he made the house, and the rafters of the house were the laws that he laid down, and he called us Haudenosaunee: the people of the Longhouse.

Now, the candidate for the clan title is brought before the Grand Council and will be judged on his merits, and they have the right of veto. If they agree, then he may take his place in Grand Council. But before that, he is turned back to the people, and they are asked if they know a reason why this man should not be a leader and hold title. Thus, the process is full circle back to the people.

Thus, the Peacemaker established the process of raising leaders for governance, and, by this process, a leader cannot be self-proclaimed. He is given his title and his duties, and his authority is derived from the people, and the people have the right to remove him for malfeasance of office.

He established the power of recall in the clanmother, and it is her duty to speak to him if she is receiving complaints from the people concerning his conduct. The clanmother shall speak to him three times, giving sufficient time between warnings for him to change his ways. She shall have a witness each time. The first will be her niece, in other words, a woman. The second shall be the partner of the chief in council or the principal leader, as the case may be. And the third and final warning comes with a man who holds no title, and he is coming for the chief's wampum and for the chief's emblem of authority, the antlers of a deer. Thus he established the power of recall vested in the people.

The leader must be free from any crime against a woman or a child.

He cannot have killed anybody and cannot have blood on his hands. He must believe in the ways of the Longhouse. His heart must yearn for the welfare of the people. He must have great compassion for his people. He must have great tolerance, and his skin must be seven spans thick to withstand the accusations, slander, and insults of the people as he goes about his duties for the people. He has no authority but what the people give him in respect. He has no force of arms to demand the people obey his orders. He shall lead by example, and his family shall not influence his judgement. He carries his title for life or until he is relieved of it by bad conduct or ill health. He now belongs to the people.

At the first council, there were 50 original leaders, and their names became offices to be filled by each succeeding generation. So, it continues up to this very day. The Great Peacemaker had established a government of absolute democracy, the constitution of the great law intertwined with the spiritual law.

"This is what prevailed upon this great Turtle Island at the first landfall of the white man. They found here in full flower, free nations guided by democratic principles, all under the authority of the natural law..."

We then became a nation of laws. The people came of their own free will to participate in the decision-making of the national council and the Grand Council. Thus, the Peacemaker instilled in the nations the inherent rights of the individual with the process to protect and exercise these rights.

Sovereignty then began with the individual, and all people were recognized to be free, from the very youngest to the eldest. It was recognized and provided for in the Great Law of Peace, that liberty and equality demanded great moral fortitude, and it was the nature of free man to defend freedom.

Thus, freedom begat freedom, and great societies of peace prevailed, guided by the leaders, the good minds. The men were restrained by moral conduct, and the family with the woman at its heart was the center of Indian societies and nations.

Now, the Peacemaker said the symbol of the Haudenosaunee shall be the great white pine with four white roots of truth extending to the four cardinal directions, and those people who have no place to go shall follow these roots back to the tree and seek shelter under the long leaves of the white pine that we shall call the great tree of peace. I shall place an eagle atop the tree to be ever-vigilant against those who shall harm this tree, and the eagle shall scream his warnings to our chiefs whose duty it is to nurture and protect this tree.

Now that this is done, the chiefs, clanmothers, and faithkeepers being raised and the Great Law being firmly established in place, he said, "I now uproot this tree and command you to throw all of your weapons of war into this chasm to be carried by the undercurrent of water to the furthest depths of the earth, and now I place this tree back over this chasm, throwing away forever war between us, and peace shall prevail."

This is what prevailed upon this great Turtle Island at the first landfall of the white man. They found here in full flower, free nations guided by democratic principles, all under the authority of the natural law, the ultimate spiritual law of the universe. This was then the land of the free and the home of the brave.

Sovereigns and sovereignty as understood by the Europeans related to the power of kings and queens, of royalty to rule men as they saw fit, to enslave human beings and control in total the lives and property of their subjects. Strange indeed it must have been for these immigrants to find a land with nothing but free people and free nations. The impact has reverberated down through history to this time. As Felix Cohen put it, "the Indian people had *Americanized* the white man."

The first treaty between the Indians and the white man took place at Skanect Dah De, the place where the pines begin—it is now called Albany, New York—in 1613 or therebouts. It was a treaty that was the grandfather of all treaties, and it was called the Guswenta or the Two Row Wampum.

That treaty established our equal rights in this land and the separate and equal coexistence on this land between our two peoples, the canoe of the Indian and the boat of the white man going down the river of life in peace and friendship forever. The last three principles were memorialized in the great silver covenant chain with the three binding us together forever, peace and friendship forever. As long as the grass grows green, as long as the water runs downhill, and as long as the sun rises in the east and sets in the west shall we hold this treaty.

This is our canoe, the Indian people, their government, and their religions. This is our brother the white man's boat, his religions, his government, and his people. Together, side by side, we go down the river of life in peace and friendship and mutual coexistence. As you note, we never come together. We are equal.

Benjamin Franklin observed these differences in government in 1770: "The care and labor of providing for artificial and fashionable wants, the sight of so many rich wallowing in superfluous plenty, whereby so many are kept poor and distressed for want, the insolence of office, and the restraints of custom all contrive to disgust the Indians with what we call civil society."

So, we now come to the process of this transference of democratic ideas and ideals from the Indian to the white man. It was a process of associations, of years of meetings, discussions, wars, and peace. Treaties became a process of relationships. Early America was steeped in Indian lore and social and political associations.

There were longstanding interrelationships between the colonies and the Indian nations that surrounded them. It was our grandfathers who took your grandfathers by the hand at the Treaty of Lancaster in 1774, and urged them to form a union such as ours so that they might prosper. It was Benjamin Franklin who took notes at that treaty and became inspired to such a union.

It was your grandfathers who said to our chiefs at German Flats in 1775 that they would now take our advice and form such a union and plant a tree of peace in Philadelphia where all could seek shelter.

Finally, it was our chiefs and leaders who first acknowledged you as a new and separate nation, independent and free, with these words, "Brothers, the whole Six Nations take this opportunity to thank you that you have acquainted us with your determination in so public a manner and we shall for the future consider you as thirteen independent states."

And they gave a white belt, a row of wampum, to commemorate this great occasion. This recognition was stated Friday, August 9, 1776, at the German Flats Treaty. This was the culmination of the long history and association with the Haudenosaunee and the immigrants who became Americans. You people went on to develop the Constitution of the United States encompassing the symbols of our constitution, the bundle of arrows symbolizing the new thirteen states, the leaves of the pine tree, and the eagle that we place upon the tree of peace. This and more we share as common history.

Brothers, we now turn our faces toward the future and continue to wish you well in your endeavors as a nation. Perhaps it would be well for you to look back again at our principles of peace, justice and equality, to grasp firmly our hand in recognition of our long association and heed the treaties that were made so long ago that these treaties may continue to thrive for our posterity as we continue down the long journey to eternity and we continue our association as government to government.

With that statement, I close the message from the Haudenosaunee, and I thank you very much for your kind attention.

10

Bringing Power Back Home:
A Blueprint From Vermont

Frank Bryan & John McClaughry

Americans' concern over the distortion of their once proudly-held constitution has affected a wide cross-section of the traditional political spectrum. Those on the political left and right alike are now engaged in the process of putting forward alternative proposals for power to be devolved to a more human scale.

Vermont, once thought to be the most conservative state in the union, is now considered to be one of the most progressive, electing socialist Bernie Sanders to Congress and, in 1988, giving Jesse Jackson the largest share of the state's Democratic convention delegates. Given this background, it is perhaps less of a surprise to find that John McClaughry (a Republican state senator and self-professed conservative) and Frank Bryan (a political science professor) propose a radical plan to bring greater democracy to Vermont by dividing it into semi-independent political units called shires.

For all its inspiring success, the American dream still lies beyond our reach. America stands as a beacon to liberty, democracy, and community. But that tradition is under challenge from the forces of centralized power—both big government's indifference to individual people's needs and big business' willful disregard of people's welfare.

Elections—the pulsing heart of American democracy—have become empty, even disgusting, spectacles. National campaigns today are issueless soap operas feasting on scandals and trivia. Their language is the language of horse races and sporting events, with commentators awaiting the next play. Disgusted voters are opting out of the whole process. If the gross national product had fallen the way voter turnout has since 1960, there would be panic in the streets. In 1990, barely a third of

Americans bothered to vote in Congressional elections. Most were disgusted with the entire political process.

Over the past quarter-century there have been many recommendations to save American politics, but they have been superficial, like giving smelling salts to a fighter whose legs have gone. We propose that American politics return to the roots of democracy. We propose that government look for a new model of politics that prizes citizenship. We propose to build a new, decentralized government structure that returns political choices to the local level, where more people can participate. As the place to build this new political process that will inspire all America, we suggest Vermont. This green state—old-fashioned and progressive at the same time—may well become the place to show us how liberty, democracy, and community can be restored to American politics.

At the very time America's democracy seems most endangered, Vermont is well-positioned to demonstrate how it can be rescued. Vermont's politics are bubbling like early sap over a new-fired arch: conventional two-party politics have become obsolete in the state. Last November, Bernie Sanders, an independent socialist, startled the nation by defeating the Republician incumbent for the state's single congressional seat. He's the first socialist elected to Congress since the 1940s. The state is brimming with non-party political organizations: the Vermont Greens, independent progressives, the American Freedom Coalition, the Rainbow Coalition, the Vermont Republican Assembly. Two independent progressives won seats in the state Senate in November.

Vermont ranked second in the nation in supporting the independent presidential candidacy of John Anderson in 1980, and Burlington elected Sanders mayor four times. He has now been replaced by Peter Clavelle, elected on the same independent Progressive ticket. In 1988 Vermont, the whitest state in America, sent to the Democratic National Convention more delegates committed to Jesse Jackson than to any other candidate. Walter Shapiro, a senior editor of *Newsweek*, has written that Vermont's politics are clearly different and that what makes them different is not conservatism. Yet "liberal" or "left" doesn't exactly sum up Vermont's new politics either.

Vermont is physically in the past and technologically in the future. It leapfrogged America's urban-industrial period and landed smack in the Information Age. It is still green. Unfettered by the baggage of urban-industrialism and free of the problems associated with it, Vermont nevertheless is among the leading states on measures of technological advancement. Those who live here enjoy a blending of past and future. We can feel the spirit of earlier Yankee and Iroquois inhabitants. We can imagine the merging of old values and new technologies.

Vermont is an ideal setting, too, because it is still a governable place. With half a million people scattered over a granite wedge of field and forest about twice the size of Connecticut, it is small enough to be politically manageable. Vermont can't save the world, but it can save itself and by its example show the United States how to get its democracy back. Working things out in a small place first is far preferable to banging one's head against the wall in a large system.

"Aristotle observed that the scale of a state should not be so great that its inhabitants cannot know one another."

In Vermont, community still lives. There is no agreement, of course, on what is actually meant by the often-used term *community*, but some characteristics appear in nearly every discussion of the subject. Community generally means people who interact at a personal level; have shared identity, values, and traditions, sense an organic bond to one another; possess the power to make many decisions about their common lives; and feel a responsibility for extending mutual aid to their fellows in need. Community, in its geographic sense, requires human scale—a scale that human beings can understand and cope with. As Aristotle observed, the scale of a state should not be so great that its inhabitants cannot know one another's character. Most important, the preservation of community requires that decisions about things that matter be made by the people affected.

In Vermont, as in the rest of the country, the idea of community has recently been weakened by trends toward centralization, mobility, mass culture, and social disintegration. But even so, Vermont remains the first place in America to go for those seeking to discover and preserve what remains of authentic community life in the 20th century. The hills are still alive with the sound of town and village, of neighborhood, corner, and place.

Vermont has largely maintained its democratic institutions. The state legislature is large and non-professional. Fewer than 10 percent of its members are lawyers, one of the lowest ratios in America. The judiciary has maintained its tradition of including citizen "side judges" on the bench. The most important institution of Vermont's democracy, however, is town government. Two hundred and thirty-six of Vermont's 246 units of government are towns in which the "executive" is a three- or five- member board and the "legislative branch" is the legendary town meeting.

The Resurrection Of The Shire

To combat giantism, preserve our liberties, reinvigorate our democracy, and reunite our communities, we propose the creation of *shires* throughout Vermont—new units of local government to which most of the powers of the state will be handed over. The shires—a name borrowed from the small-scale governing units of Old England—will allow people an accessible forum to express their most heartfelt ideas of community needs.

To achieve this, Vermont must change more radically than any other American state has ever changed. The state government will become unrecognizable by present standards. While the authority for laws that must be uniform (environmental and civil rights regulations, for example) will continue to be administered on the state level, the great bulk of spending programs (education, welfare, mental health, and even roads) will be handled by the new shire governments.

These shires are not designed as *more* government. They will represent the same amount of government we have now, but redistributed from Montpelier (our capital) to St. Johnbury, Rutland, Wilmington, Canaan, etc. We want more democracy in the government, not more government in the democracy.

The shires will be independent political units, accountable directly to their own people. They will be governed by a body elected by the people, and each one will have an independent revenue base that is adequate to its needs.

"We want more democracy in the government, not more government in the democracy."

These new shires will embody many key principles of democracy, many of which are currently missing from U.S. government at the local, state, and national levels.

- Government efficiency must never be pursued in a way that inhibits input from local citizens. All too often, when democratic control conflicts with plans for administrative efficiency, democracy is *automatically* precluded.
- The size of governing bodies must be permitted to float free and seek its own best level. At present, governments are encouraged (and often forced) upward in size but never allowed downward. The question of whether a locality is *big* enough to provide a welfare *system*, for instance, must be changed to this: Is the unit

small enough to provide the human *context*, without which attempts to care for the needy fail due to bureaucratic depersonalization?

- Democracy depends on people well-versed in the principles of citizenship. These can only be learned through taking part in human-scale institutions. Direct democracy is a requirement, not a luxury.
- Subdividing policy-making institutions into a multiplicity of one-purpose bodies (school boards, solid-waste authorities, planning commissions) creates a puzzling web that discourages people's participation. Democracy is lost to the tyranny of complexity. The size of jurisdictions must be reduced to the point where the connections between, say, highways and schools become understandable and manageable.

This decentralized political system abandons the way of government currently in favor: education by standardized tests, welfare by mailbox, police protection by radio, and health care by strangers.

The power of the state and national government as the protector of the environment and guarantor of basic civil rights and liberties will be preserved. There is also a need for state presence in other concerns that transcend local boundaries, such as transportation, disease control, information gathering, and technical assistance. But even in areas such as transportation, there should be a substantial shift of power to the shires. If, when travelling through Vermont, one encounters variations in the quality of the roads, that is the price one pays for democracy.

"To reinvigorate democracy we propose the creation of new small-scale government units called *shires*."

In all areas where lawmaking is shared between state and shire, the *administration* of policy should be at the shire level. In this way citizens will be required to do the *work* of government as well as make the decisions. An example of how this might work would be the creation of a new local post in most communities—the environmental constable, a local citizen with the power to poke around the shire and make sure laws designed to keep the countryside clean are being obeyed. With the shires in place, a whole range of administrative services now run by the state will become the work of local people.

Beyond the emotionally satisfying activity of self-government itself, several steps can be taken to establish a strong community identity in the new shires. Foremost among these steps is the creation of shire symbols. In front of the shire's public buildings, its assembly hall, town halls, schools, and community centers, will fly the unique and colorful shire flag. The shire colors will be emblazoned on its road signs and on

Seven Decentralist Strategies

Carol Moore

1 ACHIEVE CONSENSUS ON COMMON PRINCIPLES: A minimum basic agreement is required among decentralists of all stripes on philosophy and strategy. Observe the "Three Key Principles:" the search for truth, the freedom to live in light of one's truth, and nonviolent conflict resolution over different visions of truth.

The political goals should be: the creation of institutions based on womens' values and needs as well as mens'; the freedom to create autonomous communities (which may network and confederate regionally to resolve common problems and conflicts) even if it means seceding from or breaking up current nation-states; consensus-oriented deomocracy within these communities and within the regional networks and confederations they form; the institution of nonviolent conflict resolution, sanctions and defense; and the abolition of nation states. Strategy should be *radical*, emphasizing withdrawal of consent from the nation state through civil disobedience and non-cooperation and the right to secession—*not* taking power. Strategies should be *nonviolent*, to allow maximum participation by everyone, to prevent macho males from dominating, and to gain the sympathy of the masses while preventing an orgy of government violence against resisters.

2 EMPHASIZE CONSCIOUSNESS AND PROCESS: Radical and permanent change will only come from a raising of individual consciousness and an improvement in our processes of relating with one another. These are basic to restructuring our political institutions. We must learn to act from higher consciousness (tolerance, acceptance, cooperation, love) and not lower consciousness (judgementalness, fear, dominance, anger, competitiveness). Men and women must free themselves from old sex stereotypes to become their fullest selves. Group processes should be open and honest, equalitarian, consensus-seeking and freely utilize mediation and conflict resolution techniques. Abusive and violent individuals must be dealt with firmly and swiftly.

3 EDUCATE TOWARDS CRITICAL MASS: Repeat the message in every possible context in order to build a critical mass of awareness and activism that will lead

the shirts of the shire athletic teams.

Symbols of proud local history will abound. Each shire will have its monuments to commemorate shire residents or even sad events in the shire's history. Small corner parks or crossroads commons will bear the

---

eventually to a totally decentralist political culture. Educational efforts will include both standard forums like publications, study groups, lectures, the arts, and third party campaigns *and* education through action as described below.

4 *ORGANIZE LOCALLY/BUILD COMMUNITY:* This is most consistent with the decentralist goal, easiest and cheapest to organize, and allows us to start creating our alternatives immediately. We must work towards restructuring local governments to make them more participatory, more consensus-oriented, more accountable and more nonviolent. We must instill a sense of place and love of community as replacements for nationalism and patriotism.

5 *CREATE ALTERNATIVE INSTITUTIONS:* These would include: alternate communications networks of publications, telephone trees, computer networks, film and video distribution, legitimate and pirate radio and television broadcasting; alternate trade networks of businesses, individuals and organizations using trade exchanges or alternate currencies; voluntary alternatives to necesary services that have been co- opted by nation states; "shadow" or "parallel" community governments and confederations; new alternative communities.

6 *PREPARE FOR NONVIOLENT RESISTANCE/SECESSION:* Learn and practice nonviolent organizing and action by working with peace, environmental, tax resistance and social justice groups actually practicing it, meanwhile teaching them about decentralist alternatives. Organize own actions around issues of local importance. Begin coordinated campaigns of community secession from the nation-state. While these will initially be merely symbolic, they will be educational and inspirational. Since we will remain nonviolent, any government violence against us can only win public sympathy.

7 *RECOGNIZE ALTERNATE SCENARIOS AND BE OPPORTUNISTIC:* How fast decentralists move from the constructive program to resistance and secession depends on how skilfully we promote our ideas and on objective circumstances. While "gradual/reformist" scenarios are possible, more likely are "crisis" scenarios in which escalating economic, political and military crises radicalize people and open them to decentralist alternatives. And it is always possible we'll have a "post-catastrophe" scenario of *de facto* decentralization through ecological and economic collapse and world war. We should not be shy about sizing opportunities to promote our alternatives.

IN SUM: There's a lot to do and not much time to do it. So *let's get going!!*

names of citizens distinguished for their learning, achievements, or long service to the shire community.

We hope that shire citizens will enthusiastically volunteer to hold positions of civic responsibility or community self-help. It might be as an apprentice to the pound keeper, or a trumpeter in the shire band, or manager of the shire computer bulletin board. It would not be compulsory for a new citizen to choose a mode for making a contribution to the shire, but it would be expected that he or she do so.

With domestic affairs returned to the people in their shires, Vermont's state government will be free to address the other issues that must have its attention in the coming century. The *range* of state government activities will be drastically curtailed, but not necessarily the *amount* of activities. The new state government—crisp, efficient, and innovative— will maintain the purity of the environment, establish Vermont as a new actor in global affairs, and help coordinate relations among the shires, and between the shires and itself.

A new Agency of Vermont Affairs will take bold steps to increase Vermont's influence—including its emphasis on decentralized government—beyond its own borders. Within this agency, the Office of Global Involvement (OGI) will administer policy set by the state legislature in world trade, international cultural exchanges, technology sharing, and initiatives to promote world understanding and development. A prime responsibility of the OGI will be the management and expansion of programs like Vermont's people-to-people project with Honduras, begun many years ago.

As Vermonters restore their liberty, community, and democracy, perhaps others can learn from us. Our dream is that Vermont will meet its own challenge and thereby provide the nation with the hope it now so desperately needs.

11

Shadow Government

George Tukel

A typically bioregional response to the absence of local control in our government structures has been to simply get on with creating alternative structures, rather than waiting interminably for the powers-that-be to respond and "grant" such power to communities. Consequently, the idea of watershed councils, regional gatherings and broader, even continent-wide, bioregional congresses has gradually taken hold in recent years.

An east coast bioregionalist who has contributed significantly to this process, George Tukel here explains his view of alternative political institutions—or how to proceed with devolving power, without waiting for official approval...

Wildness and sustainability, as mother and offspring, speak together: that a place, before anything else, is alive, and that human participation can take a stand for and enhance or devastate that life.

It is this awareness that identifies an emerging land-based culture. A culture of reinhabitation that has come to realize that new frameworks of exchange are necessary: ones that provide adequately for a human community fully integrated into local natural systems.

Anyone living with their eyes open and with sensitivity to the industrial damage being done to people and places has to ask what is the best position to help build a wild and sustainable today and tomorrow. How to establish the alternatives that connect to a deeper, more original sensibility within the community? By playing the chords beyond power politics while addressing need.

Common sense points to reinhabitation riding the crest of two waves at once. To ensure the future, it has to be *effective* within the present array of industrial institutions and exchanges. For example, a sustainable agriculture, grounded in soil building and a growing technology not infected with fossil fuels, must be competitive in the marketplace.

Second, reinhabitation should be an *example* of what the future could be now. Why not re-see and re-invent the Hudson Valley farm as a small scale food-producing village? Owned cooperatively by, let's say, 10-30 people, a working farm of 60-250 acres, with sound buildings, could be the setting for diverse and complimentary activities. The farm would be kept in production with crops harvested for village consumption as well as for sale to local restaurants, food stands, co-ops, and city outlets. A cottage industry, for example, pressing apples for juice or cider or making local cheeses (this being apple and dairy country), would round out the possibilities that met the dual demands of good work and income generation. The village, as an organism, could be a model of eco-design: mimicking the way that natural systems use energy and resources to achieve ongoing health, stability and efficiency.

What if these two waves crossed each other? What could their meeting offer as advice?

• It's got to be do-able. No sense in wasting time.

• Environmentally sound land-use in support of sustainability is the rule and not the exception.

• Jefferson had it right: decentralized, prosperous and democratic communities are those which best resist outside authority and manipulation. Energy supply, food availablity and material usage should support self-reliance, not undermine it.

• Production and the exchange of goods and services can help maintain the life net of the numerous communities within the watershed, say, by allowing rivers to clean themselves without the presence of toxins or aquiring framing lumber from regenerating forests via local sawmills.

• Decision-making should reflect and in turn shape the identity of a wild culture, a culture guided by mutual aid and natural regeneration.

Organizations could be created that heed this advice to encourage bioregional exchange; that make clear the change from the late industrial priorities of power and growth to the human species' perceptions of wild and sustainable; to embody the shift in communities from artificial political domains to life-places, and that allow for loyalty and grace in commitment. These are organizations which could operate as a shadow government for reinhabitants.

Watershed Councils

Why watershed?
Because you can see all of it happening: touch it, smell it. Because the size and natural organization of watersheds corresponds to people

living there as natives, not as occupants. Watershed. It makes sense. A specific geographical area to infinitely know and identify with, given character by the drainage basins of streams, creeks and rivers. All moving water. Water which has scraped, carved, and littered to create soil and landform. Held together and animated by sunlight, plants, animals, nutrients and minerals blend together into an ongoing ecological process, and each blend is one-of-a-kind.

Marry sun and water in the home of landform and the child is watershed. And you are a part of it, from season to season, from year to year. The biology of the human species is intimate with the local ecology, and that's the way it's always been. Our species' senses and intellect allow us a unique view of the natural order, flesh knowing flesh.

This includes living and seeing—up close—the effects of human activities on the entire life community. If the water upstream is spoiled by garbage or if pesticides have polluted groundwater supplies, everyone (you, the beaver, your family, the bacteria in the soil) will be poisoned by it. This is probably the best reason why watershed groups (let's call them Councils in honor of the rich, direct and vibrant oratory style that characterized the decision-making meetings of the First Peoples of the area) are best suited to look after the health of the watershed which, after all, is the daily work of reinhabitation.

"Jefferson had it right: decentralized, prosperous and democratic communities are those which best resist outside authority and manipulation."

Reinhabitation exists first where people can create their own forms of exchange, both ceremonial and economic, outside of the industrial. The stage and style of drama (and some of the actors) change, though, when the daily work moves from the household and neighborhood to more public concerns, like institutional and economic alternatives. That's where the Watershed Council comes in.

Notice how non-professional volunteer environmental groups spring up, almost spontaneously, to contend with the threats of car culture to their homes, and see how tenacious they can be. (That's the wild speaking.) Being issue-oriented, these groups tend to wax and wane in response to what is most immediately pressing. But what is important is their character—place-located, tough, dug-in, friendly. If we take this character, join it with a practice of sustainability, make it forward-looking and add to it a good measure of savvy, we have a picture of what a

Watershed Council could be: a move past environmentalism to an ecological populism; reinhabitants seeking full membership in the life communities where they live.

Okay, what would be the actual concerns of Watershed Councils? At present, the planning and shape of human settlements, usually defined by market forces constrained by building codes, zoning regulations and environmental controls, has more to do with the profits of developers and contractors and the politics of land usage than it does with individual and community well-being, human services, and the integrity of local ecosystems. Painting in broad strokes, Watershed Councils would seek to turn this pattern upside down. Communities can begin to see themselves as aligning human requirements with natural ones.

Looking at it from a more nuts and bolts side of things, Councils could be working first to remove land from the allowed vulgarities of the marketplace and to support reinhabitants in their practice of sustainability. Of course, Watershed Councils aren't against people making a living off the land. Actually, that's what they want most. Just so long as it's done without excessive pain to natural surroundings while maintaining a regenerative resource base, as in preserving farmland for those coming up later on.

Practical steps, though, can be taken by Watershed Councils to accomplish this while breathing new life into the heritage of local land ethics. Witness the European legal tradition of holding land for the common good and the Native American practices of loyalty, service and thankfulness to the land.

First of all, Watershed Councils can help get good people appointed or elected to planning boards (any strong-willed meeting addicts out there?). The usual land-use decision-making framework—zoning regulations and their application—are the responsibility of planning boards. Better there be five-acre zoning than one-quarter or one-half acre, better a concentration of necessary development as opposed to spreading it over farmland and ecologically sensitive areas.

Better still, though, is to remove the long term land-use decision-making from the politics of planning boards altogether. The most immediate way is for small groups of people with strong land ethics to marshall their financial resources and buy available parcels as they come up—for example, farms where our small villages could be created. Deed restrictions could then be reasoned out, safeguarding the natural patterns of the place while keeping the land productive. Working on a broader basis, Watershed Councils can promote and assist in the creation of Community Land Trusts: local, not-for-profit, organized and run by citizens. They provide the time and place where practitioners of sustainability swap information, ideas, and ways of getting things done.

Watershed Councils are already working hard to set the foundations for community life which, like the natural world, provides and renews at the same time. By putting all life before property and profit, Councils become integral to a cultural politics that locates wildness—a felt sense of place—as the basis of a new social contract that does not rely on power, fear, or manipulation for its legitimacy and effectiveness. For those whose values have matured past the industrial and institutional, Watershed Councils have become the local leg of a biocentric shadow government.

But things are going on in the next valley, upriver or throughout the estuary, that are important to local resiliency and flexibility. What happens when watershed sustainability and restoration require talk that is more than a short drive away? Or when Watershed Councils have to speak about issues, and a phone call won't do?

That's when it's time for Forest Communities to come together to move on matters of common cause.

Forest Communities Gather

At a visible scale between watershed and bioregion, Forest Communities, whose boundaries are based on landform and plant life, make for unforced reciprocity between watersheds within Forest Communities and between Forest Communities within the Hudson estuary. And as watersheds allow for day-to-day specific action, Forest Communities allow for planning and cooperative effort about maintaining a diverse and healthy biota (which includes the human species, seen by some as endangering, seen by others as endangered).

Take your movie camera to the lookout on Highway 44-55 and attach the zoom lens of your dreams. Point it out over the valley, zoom in, and study the plants, wildlife, or whatever might be happening. Start to turn the lens slowly. As you pull back to a wider angle, watersheds transform into Forest Communities, putting into focus needed context for local planning and action. This transformation results in ecological continuity, a continuity that allows an evolving picture of Forest Community life to correct and be corrected by activities within watersheds.

How could we film it? Start with a natural resources inventory as the setting. An inventory would list and describe native plants and animals, climate, soils, geology, water resources, air quality, population densities and land-use. The result? An accurate picture of human and natural intervention on the landscape so we know where we stand.

The main character in our movie would be the development of sustainable communities through an understanding of carrying capacity. Carrying capacity represents a dynamic balance point for evaluating development alternatives and ecological costs and benefits. The story line would be in integrating a resources inventory with carrying capacity to provide the information to assess the conditions of watersheds and their development in their physical, biological and technological states. Forest Gatherings would seem a good place to produce this movie, among other things. Because people are not only talking about reinhabitation, they are making a go of it, hands-on, being practical and visionary, making the choices that affect their livelihoods and life styles, and they need each other's help.

"A Watershed Council could be a move past environmentalism to an ecological populism; reinhabitants seeking full membership in the life communities where they live."

Watershed Councils, with so much in common, would have a lot to share at Forest Gatherings. Besides catching up on the latest with old and new friends, local peoples could exchange information on what works and what doesn't: the tractor implements best for soil and yield; low-cost energy and housing advances and how to explain them to building inspectors; the legal techniques best for stopping runaway suburbanization of rural lands; building community consensus on possible sustainable futures. If Watershed Councils are to move with a steady gait, combining workability and well-being, they need straight talk on techniques and planning.

Forest Gatherings could also be the time and place to make plans and scheme about how to best bring these new community structures into the world. Common effort has a better chance of working out if there is an initial face-to-face sharing of needs and ideas with time to articulate, mull over and clearly define matters. This could be the general drift of things when Forest Communities get together as distinct ecological regions, or group together for a Hudson Estuary Bioregional Congress.

It would be wonderful and critical to re-establish the city/country connection via the tradition of farming close to urban areas. Connecting city and country in day-to-day dealings, to provide food and financial stability, will mean a commitment to bioregional integrity: working with sustainable solutions and taking pride in the effort. It will also mean answering questions that cross and include watersheds. Where are the growers of food upriver? Where are outlets for buyers downriver? How can they be tied together with a Hudson River-based transportation system?

Lurking in the background are other issues just waiting to burst forward. How best to protect farmland from development? It's irrelevant to talk about what crops are best to harvest when there is no land to grow them on. Or how best to restore traditional landing points, gone to seed, on the Hudson, for food drops to farmers' markets.

At Forest Gatherings, farmers, co-op members, alternative transportation advocates and wholesalers could sit around the table talking about how to make food self-sufficiency a reality. The same for energy, water, or shelter. Tie individual activities into adaptive strategies for reinhabiting the Hudson estuary. Upriver-downriver for the long haul.

12

Watershed Stewardship: The Village Of Hazelton Experience

Alice Maitland & Doug Aberley

The heart of the decentralist vision is the democratic municipality, a body comprised by the people and acting for and on behalf of the people. Rarely, however, do contemporary municipalities match up to this high ideal. They are, instead, constrained by their mandate to focus upon a relatively narrow set of concerns, and the major decisons impacting their immediate environments are made elsewhere, in distant capitals and boardrooms.

Remarkably, the tiny mid-northern town of Hazelton in British Columbia has gone beyond the usual and conventionally allowable jurisdictional limits of a municipality. Arguing that the welfare of the town and its local populace requires its active participation in the stewardship of regional resources, Hazelton is blazing a new trail in the field of watershed management. The process by which the town has done this is almost as significant as the outcome to date. Architects of this "upstart" municipal revolution, the authors are mayor and town planner respectively of the town of Hazelton.

In January of 1990 something special happened in a small community located at the junction of two large northern rivers. At a municipal council meeting in Hazelton, British Columbia, elected representatives unanimously agreed that a unique initiative must be undertaken if the community and surrounding region were ever to enjoy a stable prosperity. Responsibility for management of natural resources must be removed from the mandate of central governments, bureaucracies, and large corporations. Jurisdiction over new techniques of sustainable natural resource stewardship must be devolved to local and regional control.

From this understanding grew one community's effort to achieve total reorganization of the way in which natural resources are stewarded in British Columbia: the *Framework For Watershed Stewardship* is a document which proposes fundamental changes in the manner in which B.C. forests are perceived and regulated. It evolved from Hazelton's unique location and setting, and from its history with forest-management-related activities. This is the story of how the Framework was conceived, and has now been revised.

Hazelton And The "Politics Of Place"

The site of present day Hazelton was first inhabited by clans of the Gitksan nation well over 5,000 years ago. Settled by Europeans in 1866, Hazelton maintained an aura of uniqueness and isolation. Until well after World War II it was impossible for a stranger to arrive in the area without the knowledge of everyone in the community. Cupped in a hollow of the mountains that surround three river valleys, generations of inhabitants jealously guarded the quality of life and spirit they had found. Hospitality was rich and warm, but only when guests came to carefully share the plenty that flourished here.

Hazelton is currently a community of 456 persons and is the center of what is now known as the Upper Skeena region of Northwest British Columbia. Situated 500 miles north of Vancouver and 200 miles inland from Prince Rupert, the community retains a connection to its history and the surrounding land that is rare and unmistakable. The region's population is 6,000 persons, half of Gitksan and Wet'suwet'en descent, and half of pioneer Euro-Canadian ancestry. There has never been a development project in the region of a size that has brought in an overwhelming component of transients or of homogenized southern culture.

The Gitksan and Wet'suwet'en claim a 20,000 square mile territory around Hazelton and are renowned for the degree to which their traditional culture remains a vital force. Despite the setback of a recent decision in the Supreme Court of B.C. denying legal basis to this claim, current hereditary chiefs of the Gitksan and Wet'suwet'en nations continue to pursue a landmark court challenge that will redefine important aspects of local control and self-governance. It is common to hear aboriginal languages spoken on the streets of the community as issues such as sovereignty and resource management are discussed with an intensity born of decades of struggle.

Pioneer families who have inhabited the area since the 1860s are equally tenacious. They have lived many generations in the Hazelton area and have refined a very unpredictable "politics of place." They do not easily fall into the category of being either "left" or "right," but are influenced by a love of community and deep suspicion of change and outside authority. The joining of these two unique cultures has marked the Hazelton area as a rare region capable of and willing to guide its own affairs.

There are 15 small settlements in the Upper Skeena region represented by nearly 200 elected community association or local government officials, and 76 Gitksan and Wet'suwet'en House chiefs. The politics of these communities runs from arch-conservative to direct-action militancy. Sometimes it is perceived that the word anarchy was invented to describe the curious blend of cooperation and friction that is the hallmark of local political interaction. The nature of this interaction is such that there is always debate between local jurisdictions regarding how the region should be governed and developed. At worst there is bickering, at best the area is the most politically progressive region in B.C.

"The Village of Hazelton has a reputation for pursuing initiatives designed to increase the stability and independence of rural communities and regions."

The Village of Hazelton is one of two municipalities in the region. The community has been in existence since 1866 and was incorporated as a municipality in 1956. Bounded by the Skeena River, the town enjoys a historic and scenic setting. The town Council is made up of a mayor and four aldermen, three of whom are currently of Gitksan ancestry and two of pioneer heritage. There are three full-time staff. The Village of Hazelton has a reputation for pursuing initiatives designed to increase the stability and independence of rural communities and regions.

Watershed Events For The Town

The Upper Skeena forest is a transition ecosystem located between coastal and inland climatic influences. So-called "decadent" hemlock predominates. Because of this "non-economic" characteristic, industrial logging came into the region at a relatively late date. The early development of the Hazelton area forest industry was extremely slow and cautious. The Ministry of Forests was represented by as few as three employees who knew the country well and oversaw the harvesting and manufacturing of cedar poles, railway ties, firewood, and logs used in the operation of family operated sawmills. Impacts of timber extraction were *un*-frightening and negligible as openings in the forest were small, and there was minimal use of machinery.

In the late 1950s, family-owned tenures were bought out by a large company. Family-owned "bush" mills were shut down and a greatly increased harvest was funnelled to a new sawmill. The sawmill went through a number of closures, fires, and changes of ownership. Logging and trucking contractors from outside the region began to undercut the lowest bids that could be made by local companies. Clearcuts appeared on hillsides, and lakes were logged to their shorelines. Moonscapes were left where lush forests had been. Wages were high, but the uncertainty of boom and bust employment cycles was devastating. Traditional economies were largely abandoned as reliance on trapping and other subsistence pursuits could not coexist with the incessant march of clearcuts.

The community's relationship with industrial forestry soured. When the central sawmill burned in the late 1960s, Hazelton's town council took the first step towards diversifying the local economy and away from total reliance on the forest industry. Out of wide discussion that took place during this period came two firm goals. The first was that the community would commit its energy to securing a voice in the management of area forests. The second resolve was to develop the unique cultural and scenic attributes of the region as a world-class visitor destination.

In 1969 Hazelton helped to establish 'Ksan Historic Indian Village and Museum. 'Ksan's museum, carving school, and meeting facilities quickly became the focus for a strengthening of local Native culture. Throughout the 1970s, awareness grew of local capabilities to better govern and develop the Upper Skeena region. Results of this widespread cultural resurgence were the 1977 organization of the Gitksan-Carrier Tribal Council (now renamed Gitksan-Wet'suwet'en Hereditary Chiefs), and a growing awareness in the pioneer community that central governments were not properly stewarding local resources. Concepts such as empowerment, local control, and cultural pride were reasserted and practiced.

At this time, the Village Council addressed forest management issues on an emergency-by-emergency basis, with little positive result. Annual Allowable Cuts were increased, the town watershed was poorly logged, the public advisory process disbanded, poor utilization allowed, and a host of forestry-related disappointments experienced. There was growing realization that while the municipality must remain involved in local forest issue debates, there must also be energy dedicated to creating a model for local control of resource management.

In the early 1980s two important initiatives occurred. First, the Village Council included in a draft community plan the goal of practicing stewardship over the entire Upper Skeena watershed. This goal was an acknowledgement that the area which sustained the community far exceeded town boundaries.

Second, a community questionnaire was executed that saw two-hour interviews done in every Hazelton household. Questions were included which asked resident opinion about resource management issues. Council believed that this detailed understanding of community concern was necessary to insure that expanded political action represented community opinion. With this mandate Council became involved in a greatly expanded number of innovative forestry-related actions.

Asserting Local Control

In the mid 1980s, the Forest Advisory Committee process had degraded into a frustrating exercise that was both poorly attended and managed, and in 1986 the Kispiox Forest District Forest Advisory Committee was disbanded. As a replacement, the Village of Hazelton proposed a quarterly "report card" that would gauge the ongoing performance of the Ministry of Forests. By giving figures for area logged, plantation survival, stumpage revenue, etc., it was felt that the community would be able to react if any of these parameters signalled alarming increase or decline. The Ministry of Forests made an attempt to implement the report card, but found that their system of management did not generate the area-specific data that was required.

In 1988, when a local sawmill closed down, a 500-person protest march closed the Yellowhead Trans-Canada Highway. It was an amazing sight to see the R.C.M.P. (Royal Canadian Mounted Police) take video evidence of Hazelton's senior 69 year-old alderman as he rode in the town firetruck that was leading the march. This and other actions brought a unique gesture by the company shutting the sawmill. The mill property was sold to the community for one dollar. The mill was then resold for $325,000 to a local mill operator who was expanding into value-added manufacturing of low quality logs. The money was distributed to support recreation facilities in every community in the region.

Later, the Village monitored the award of a forest license in an area north of Hazelton. When the award was made to Prince George companies, apparently for political reasons, the Village asked for an Ombudsman's investigation. The Ombudsman's report found that Cabinet had illegally usurped the legal responsibility of the chief forester to make the timber license award. The Village is investigating legal action against the Ministry of Forests for a variety of offences stemming from this incident.

Finally the Village instigated a process by which property taxes from the area's only large sawmill, which is located outside of municipal boundaries, could be collected for use by local municipalities. This negotiation was made in cooperation with the sawmill company. Collection of $60,000 annually is now made possible by the extension of the boundary of New Hazelton 17 kilometres down Highway 16 in a long "umbilical cord." The money collected is then divided between Hazelton and New Hazelton for recreation and cultural projects.

Despite these and other actions, and despite Village participation in Local Resource Use Plans, Advisory Planning Committees, Resource Management Plans, Management and Working Plans and other forestry initiatives, frustration with lack of reform in the forest Ministry and industry grew.

In 1989 a third major community questionnaire was carried out, this time including a greater number of forest management queries than previously included. The results of these questions showed 80-plus percent dissatisfaction with forest management as practiced in the region. At this point Village Council met and agreed that it was no longer enough to simply protest single issues and participate in an ever increasing number of forest ministry initiatives.

The Forest Industry Charter Of Rights

On 19 January 1990 the Village of Hazelton sent out 200 copies of a proposed *Forest Industry Charter of Rights*. This document was a first attempt to assemble a set of principles and rules of practice for sustainable, or "new" forestry in British Columbia. By appending these precepts to the existing Forest Act, it was put forward by the Village that current confrontations between citizens and communities of British Columbia and the forest industry would largely cease. It was time to link carrying capacity of forests with extraction levels. It was time to link community stability with management regimes. It was time to confront the central government with a detailed and aggressive alternative to the status quo. The 30 principles in the *Charter* were a first expression of this alternative.

Response to the *Charter* was overwhelming. Well over 100 further copies of the document have been requested by community groups, forestry companies, the media, and concerned residents of a score of rural communities.

The *Charter* has been adopted wholly, or in principle, by eleven municipalities and regional districts. In several cases detailed critiques were prepared by municipal forestry committees who obviously spent many hours reviewing *Charter* tenets. Nearly every other local government in British Columbia considered the *Charter* and referred it to industry, municipal associations, or their own Minister of Forests for consideration.

Forest industry reaction has run the gambit from extremely critical (Council of Forest Industries); to condescending (B.C. Association of Registered Professional Foresters); to constructive (Westar Timber, REPAP Inc.). The general tone of industry response was that recent changes to forest management practice made most sections of the *Charter* redundant. Proposed structural changes to forest management as reflected in the *Charter* (such as community control, etc.) received no industry comment because these concerns were felt by industry to be too complex, or political, to address.

Provincial response to the *Charter* followed the general tone expressed by the forest industry. It was stated by the Ministry of Forests that most points raised in the *Charter* had already been adequately addressed by existing government and industry initiatives.

"We are more determined than ever to continue with our goal of expanding municipal jurisdiction into the realm of watershed politics and management."

It was the opinion of Village Council that the forest industry and Ministry of Forests only responded to the *Charter* because public pressure made a response necessary. The content of this response was devoid of any resolve to address the central issue that the *Charter* raises: local control of ecologically regulated resource harvests. The lesson learned by Council was that central governments and large companies would likely never respond with enthusiasm to demands that would drastically reduce their power and wealth.

The most gratifying response has been from citizens and community groups. While most replies have noted principles to add or strengthen, it is obvious that the *Charter* has had a galvanizing effect. The simple idea that the Ministry of Forests and forest industry should be bound by clear and strict rules of sustainable forest management is an idea whose time has come.

During the last twelve months, 100 written responses to the *Charter* have been received. The *Charter* has been rewritten to reflect the best of the comments received. In many cases the revisions have been minor, such as the tightening of vocabulary, or the addition of explanation. There have also been some substantial changes and additions to the organization and content of the document. These revisions reflect both critiques that were received, and Hazelton's increasing understanding of how reform of our forest industry must take place. The major revisions to the *Charter* can be summarized as follows.

1. The *Charter* has been renamed to *A Framework for Watershed Stewardship*. This major re-orientation reflects our growing belief that stewardship of forests must be managed in consort with equal treatment of other air, land, and water resources.

2. The *Framework* provides greater detail regarding: a) how the Ministry of Forests would be re-organized into a new Ministry of Natural Resources; and b) how devolution of resource management would occur to regional "Watershed Authorities." The original *Charter* left it up to the Ministry of Forests to study ways in which devolution would occur. The new *Framework* reflects the understanding that no central government agency would be likely to do an adequate job of designing its own demise.

3. The *Framework* includes a score of new sections which were suggested by reviewers of the original *Charter*. The *Framework* explains 75 principles of natural resource stewardship which fall under the general headings of administrative organization, public participation, planning process, water and air resources, biodiversity and habitat protection, forest industry, mining, parks and recreation, tourism, fish, wildlife, agriculture, transportation, urban land use, energy, and archaeological/cultural sites.

4. The "Framework" more aggressively sets out a planning process by which natural resource management will occur. This major addition is an attempt to describe a planning process that meets the needs of local communities for: a) generation and interpretation of detailed biophysical information; and b) a region-based decision-making process that is responsive to a community's sustainable development goals.

Hazelton's experience with the *Charter* and *Framework for Watershed Management* warrants several comments.

First, it has been an extremely rewarding process to go beyond the frustration of confronting only single issues of resource management. We now fully understand that community empowerment comes not only from struggling against injustice, but also from proposing viable alternatives.

Second, we have learned that there is a tremendous constituency of concerned citizens and organizations who care for the future of our province. The expressions of this concern, including the *Framework* and many other submissions we have received, offer a clear direction for reform of resource management to better reflect ecological and community development imperatives.

Third, we are more determined than ever to continue with our goal of expanding municipal jurisdiction into the realm of watershed politics and management. The future of Hazelton is based on the health and sustainable productivity of our surrounding environments and ecosystems. Every community, in British Columbia and across the continent, must become aware of this fundamental fact, and take whatever measures are necessary to conserve and steward their watershed legacies.

We will continue to seek constructive input into revisions that will make the *Framework* a better document. We understand that there are many principles yet to be added, and much debate to be had regarding the exact parameters of sustainable human land use guidelines. In the coming years we will endeavour to continue to add to the *Framework*, and periodically circulate these revisions for consideration and adoption by a widening circle of responsible local governments.

A Growing Empowerment

The energy of elected representatives in small communities is usually dedicated to making an endless succession of small decisions about utility systems, growth and decline, finances, and orchestrating a rough harmony between many differing interests. It is rare that an issue of concern to the larger continental community is pushed to prominence by a rural Town Council.

The *Framework for Watershed Stewardship* has become one of those rare issues. It has taken a great deal of time and effort to write, distribute, and revise the *Charter* and *Framework* documents. There has been harsh or condescending response from those whose interests we have threatened. There has been unease over exactly how we should formulate the structure of ecologically-responsible resource stewardship. But there has also been an empowerment which has arisen from contact with those who share our concern for sustainability, from learning how much influence our call for change can have, and from understanding the power that a citizens movement can build. We thank all those who have helped this journey from having little voice in how our resources are stewarded, to the knowledge that our call for change is alive far beyond the boundaries of our small community.

(Copies of the Framework for Watershed Stewardship can be purchased for $2.00 from Village of Hazelton, P.O. Box 40, Hazelton B.C., Canada V0J 1Y0.)

13

Community Forest Boards: Gaining Control Of Our Forests

Herb Hammond

On Canada's west coast, much of the protest about the lack of public participation in decision-making revolves around the resource industries— forestry in particular. The widespread clearcutting of forests is no longer acceptable to a more and more environmentally aware population, but up until recently, the large corporations which control the industry have divided forest workers from "environmentalists" and proceeded with business-as-usual, leaving local communities to be the losers. Yet, increasingly, these different groups are seeing that their interests are common, that the economic future of resource communities is inextricably tied to their ecological well-being through time. Subsequently, much creative thought has gone into how the forests might be better managed by local communities for a sustainable future.

Foremost among the pioneers in this field is Herb Hammond, a forester and consultant from the Kootenay region of British Columbia. In this article, he outlines the details of how community-based resource boards might function to work for the long-term interests of all.

Centralized government, centralized education, and single-interest control over British Columbia's forests have, over time, removed responsibility for the local forest from the local communities which depend upon them. Decisions which shape the destiny of local forests and the communities which depend upon them are usually made far from the forest and the community, often by corporate interests in Vancouver and, with increasing frequency, as far away as Japan.

In these instances, responsibility is much more likely to mean responsibility to a balance sheet rather than to a forest and a community of people. The forest becomes a computer printout of timber volumes. Neighbors become employment statistics. Problems come in envelopes and leave in envelopes. Responsibility to forests and people is easily abrogated. Community stability has come to mean industrial stability for those people making decisions about the use of B.C. forests.

The Structure Of Community Control

Community control of B.C.'s forests could be achieved through Community Forest Boards (CFBs) responsible for *all* forest uses within logical watershed areas. Under the direction of provincial legislation, the CFBs would carry out all planning (including field design and layout) and management for the region controlled by the Board. The Board would be responsible for preparing a land-use or forest-use plan which zones the forest to achieve balanced forest use.

Zones would be created for cultural protection, ecologically sensitive areas, fish and wildlife, trapping, wilderness, tourism and public recreation, and timber. Zoning of forests and subsequent management would be based upon a wholistic, field-based inventory of natural, social and economic factors conducted under the direction of the CFB. This inventory and zoning would form the foundation for the CFB to develop specific management plans for forest uses within each zone.

"Centralized government, centralized education, and single-interest control of our forests have, over time, removed responsibility over the local forest from the local communities which depend upon them."

Management plans for each zone or forest use would contain detailed specifications for the type of activities which are appropriate, and the standards which appropriate activities must meet. General standards and techniques for ecologically-responsible forest use contained in CFB plans would be set out in provincial legislation to ensure consistency throughout B.C. This umbrella legislation should be developed through a participatory process between central government and CFBs to ensure that standards and specifications are built from the ground up, rather than imposed from the top down.

Within the context of the general standards enshrined in provincial legislation, CFBs would have latitude to specify more detailed standards. CFBs would then proceed to allocate forest uses to various individuals and groups either through grants to non-profit forest users such as public recreation societies or forest ecology associations, or through competitive bid proposals.

CFBs would set a minimum bid acceptable for this forest use thereby ensuring that all expenses of the Board in inventorying forests, planning, and administration of a particular forest use were covered. Additional monies would be available to the communities for on-going forest management and other socio-economic needs. CFBs would also ensure that sales of various forest uses (particularly timber) would provide protected niches for individuals and small businesses.

Negotiations between CFBs and central government would be necessary to develop legislation as to how revenues from local forest uses would be shared between the provincial government and the community. The power of the CFBs may be extended to work with other local agencies such as school boards and regional districts to allocate revenues directly to these institutions rather than cycling forest-use monies through a central government and back again.

"We are past the era where a frontier ethic, which supports private owners being able to do whatever they like on their own land, is socially and ecologically acceptable."

The Boards could be established by combining the processes of election and appointment. Balanced representation would mean that the first principle of the composition of any CFB should be that all forest user groups are represented in an equitable way on the Board. Legislation should set out obvious categories of forest users to be represented on the Board, with local boards having the power to add to this representation. In addition to forest user groups, a number of people (perhaps three or four) would be elected from the community-at-large to complete the CFB.

The question of boundaries next arises, as well as the ideal number of Boards. The answer should be based upon the need for logical watershed units and workable size as a first priority.

The basic functions of the CFBs would be:

1) Complete field-based forest inventories of all natural, social, and economic factors;

2) Zoned forest use based upon comprehensive inventories and community participation;

3) Wholistic management plans for the various zones comprising the regions administered by the CFBs;

4) Allocation of forest-use rights to private individuals and organizations pursuant to the management plans;

5) Collection of revenues from allocated forest uses; and

6) Field design, layout, supervision, and evaluation of various forest activities under the wholistic management plan.

These six primary tasks would be designed, supervised, reviewed, and revised by a permanent staff in the employ of and under the direction of the CFB. In turn, this staff would hire (with the final approval of the Board) contractors and consultants to carry out specific duties and tasks within the philosophy set forth by the CFB and to standards specified by the Board.

The authority of local forest use boards should extend to all forest land, private or public, within the forest region administered by the CFB. We are past the era where a frontier ethic, which supports private owners being able to do whatever they like on their own land, is socially and ecologically acceptable. All forest landholders must recognize that forests are interconnected webs. What a private owner does on her/his land affects other ecosystems and other people.

New legislation is required to provide for the phasing out of the current tenure system and the phasing in of community control of forests, both public and private, through a system of CFBs. A philosophy of forest use, to guide community control of forests, must be clearly enshrined in the legislation, as well as the process and general standards for achieving this new philosophy of forest use.

While model legislation may be proposed from the central government, proposals should be directed to local communities to share in the decision-making involved in finalizing the legislation.

14

The Temagami Stewardship Council

Mary Laronde with Judith Harris

Nowhere is the call for local autonomy more urgent than among the native peoples of this continent. Their lands stolen and their rights abrogated, they have faced in recent years more and more incursions into their traditional territories by resource companies eager to exploit dwindling resources. In Ontario, these struggles have centred upon a place called Temagami, with environmentalists and native people joining forces to protect one of the last major wilderness areas in that province.

In April, 1990, the Teme-Augama Anishnabai (TAA) and the government of Ontario agreed in a precedent-setting Memorandum of Understanding to establish a stewardship council—an agreement later ratified by the Ontario cabinet in May, 1991. The council will provide for joint management of four townships comprising 40,000 hectares of land and water in the centre of the TAA's homeland, n'Daki-Menan. This interview with Mary Laronde—an elected representative of the Teme-Augama Anishnabai who has played a key role in managing the TAA's involvement in the Temagami Stewardship Council and is responsible for the Lands and Resources portfolio—explores what sustainability means for Temagami and how regional planning will proceed under the stewardship council. Judith Harris, a doctoral student at the University of Waterloo, conducted the interview at Bear Island, Lake Temagami, Ontario; she is investigating community-based planning alternatives arising from "new economic" theories.

Judith Harris: *The memorandum states that a stewardship council will be created for the four townships of Delhi, Acadia, Shelburne, and Canton with membership appointed 50/50 by the TAA and the Ontario government and that "no timber licences will be issued without the approval of the stewardship council." Why is timber the only resource covered in this agreement?*

Mary Laronde: Basically, there is no reason to include this statement in the agreement since stewardship means *all* uses and management of the land—land being understood as a wholistic concept, interchangeable with "the earth."

Timber has perhaps been highlighted because more than 1,000 hectares of old growth forest are located in the four townships covered under the stewardship agreement. The agreement thus is a way of looking after this political hot potato.

We were against access into this area which represents the last six percent of n'Daki-Menan not split open by resource extraction roads. The plan here was to go in and get at the last vestiges of our pine forests. For many years our position has been that areas need to be studied and understood before any heavy uses go ahead. Humans don't understand everything, so we can't just go ahead and change the natural world. I guess the specific timber reference unequivocally neutralized the existing plan to log here and defers any new decisions to the stewardship council.

The interim bilateral process referred to in the agreement specifically deals with timber management because it's the largest, most entrenched use here, so it's a spearhead for other developments. For example, one of the main benefits of logging is that it establishes roads and access to activities which the public feels are its right to enjoy. This is why timber management is something we immediately want to effect changes in because we don't agree with the attitude that the land is valueless unless there's a road and that the management practices and view of the Ministry of Natural Resources (MNR) in supplying lumber and jobs is the one and only view of forestry.

JH: *How does the stewardship council affect the TAA's land claim negotiations?*

ML: The stewardship council is one aspect of the Memorandum of Understanding and negotiations are another but they are inextricably linked. The creation of the stewardship council is based on the fact that Ontario and the TAA agree to work toward a Treaty of Coexistence and that stewardship of the land is fundamental to coexistence. The stewardship council is the working model for coexistence and it is expanding this shared jurisdictional arrangement over the balance of the area, save for areas under municipal jurisdictions and those under exclusive Teme-Augama Anishnabai jurisdiction—that will be part of treaty negotiations.

As for the land claim, per se, it is a misnomer from one point of view.

We see it as a land defense in what is ultimately a human rights issue and an issue of constitutional import: aboriginal rights. The land defense takes on many different faces or processes. The stewardship council evolved from a primarily political process. But that is greatly affected, I should think, by the legal process. However, the stewardship council and the overall agreement does not preempt the legal process which is on-going separately. The Supreme Court of Canada will hear our case sometime in 1991 and if they rule as I believe they should, we will have our legal title to n'Daki-Menan declared. In that event, as the legally recognized owners of our homeland, and possessing the jurisdictional powers that accompany that, we would still pursue a shared decision-making regime on our lands because we don't want to ram our laws down anyone's throat. We've had that choking experience since the Ontario government became interested in our natural resources around 1900, and moved in with laws and forced them on our people under the threat of arms and incarceration. Coexistence between peoples precludes this kind of undignified, oppressive behavior and this is not what we're about.

"When trade takes over the activities once performed in the home, then what you have is really a feudal system and people have become serfs."

JH: *The Brundtland Commission saw the concept of sustainable development as a means of ensuring the availability of resources for this and future genera-tions through a marriage of environmental and economic goals. In the context of Temagami how appropriate and feasible is sustainable development?*

ML: I've understood sustainable development to mean that we'll continue doing logging. That's what it means as it is put forward by the government and companies in the area...a continuance of mining and logging. But what's going on now is not sustainable. Sustainable development is too entrenched in the old economic, money system where profits are the bottom line.

It used to be that the word "economy" had nothing to do with the Toronto Stock Exchange. It meant you put something away for tomor-row. It meant you preserved berries and smoked foods. When trade takes over the activities once performed in the home, then what you have is really a feudal system and people have become serfs. For the existing form of economy to work you must first take away people's dignity. You must disempower them. People have to be tread upon for this economic system to survive.

JH: *At the Conference on Temagami held at Laurentian University in October 1989, you proposed sustainable life as an alternative to sustainable development. Could you explain what this would mean in Temagami?*

ML: Sustainable life means that the land dictates how people will use the land and this needs to be the principle we follow so we can all have certainty for the future. The shared stewardship regime, based on the principle of sustained life, will mean in Temagami that the local people, individuals and small communities, would regain power over their lives and assume responsibility for their lifestyle. Our relationship in Temagami to the land would change.

From a fiscal point of view, the government pulls out ten million dollars a year from our homeland, according to a 1983 estimate, for the use of our land—that is the whole of n'Daki-Menan. Per capita [including both native and non-native residents] they put back in the same amount. So that, on balance, the government makes no profit from resource development in our homeland. The idea that we are a drain on the public purse is ludicrous. This whole country survives on the use and abuse of Indian lands.

JH: *Does the concept of sustainable life require a fundamental change in how we view economic, environmental and regional planning?*

ML: We need greater sensitivity to "our" role, the human factor. We have to be more long-sighted for the sake of future generations. The preponderance of timber activities is archaic in this day and age...we need to provide jobs but we cannot provide them in lumber and other non-renewable resource industries at this level for an indeterminate period. If the price we pay [for development] is the cost of sustaining our way of life and our collective ability to live off the land, then the price is too high.

"The shared stewardship regime, based on the principle of sustained life, will mean in Temagami that the local people, individuals and small communities, would regain power over their lives and assume responsibility for their lifestyle."

We have to be more creative in rural and undeveloped areas. To have the same economic structure as in developed areas and to expect that n'Daki-Menan is on its way to becoming a region modelled on southern Ontario is death to this land. You can't eat money.

With regard to regional government, the model of government that we were looking at in 1983 was for what I would call "area" government as opposed to the type of regional government found in Sudbury. It is intended to encourage pluralism. It is based on a new political order and represents one way of looking at shared jurisdiction. It illustrates our desire to accommodate and provide for autonomy for communities and individuals on our land.

In thinking about options for n'Daki Menan, we've been able to sense from the public that they feel we are able to look after the land. There are people who are not opposed to using Indian land on our terms. We feel that a 50/50, local/provincial shared-jurisdictional arrangement could give voice and representation to the full range of interests. Then perhaps the TAA would not become extinct and our land would not be destroyed.

Some people do accept this idea and even our jurisdiction over this land. Because they're not opposed, they seem to see it as a more equitable way of looking after the land.

The trees here take 120 years to grow and MNR has a 20-year plan. Even at that, they go in and cut but they don't have any plan at that time for regeneration. Their silviculture prescription comes *after* the cutting. It's impossible to regenerate white pine because it needs cover. MNR's silviculture is too homogeneous. Their approach is one of damage control. They find out they have made a mistake in cutting, and then they say, well, there is nothing that can be done and this area is beyond recovery. So it goes with poplar and birch.

In the stewardship area, activity will initially have to be highly regulated. Some canoe sites will have to be closed. We're losing the soil on the campsites at these points. We need to look at ways of regulating use and limiting the number of boats—large boats, sea-doos and houseboats which anchor in areas where loons nest. There's a lot of overuse. We have 10,000 years of experience living on and managing these lands. We are totally sensitive to it. It is our mother.

JH: *What essentially were the intentions of the Teme-Augama Anishnabai when the TAA erected the blockade on the Red Squirrel Road on Remembrance Day, 1990? In what ways have these concerns been addressed?*

ML: The immediate goal at that time was to prevent the road from being built. The road is there but it is closed and it is not completed. It's impassable and one section has sunk.

Beyond that we now do have recognition of our presence on these lands and acceptance of our right to be a major part of the decision-making process on these lands. For the first time, the government has responded to the fundamental realities of indigenous peoples in their homeland: that we are separate and distinct from the Canadian "melting pot;" that we have original title; and that they derived their land title from us. Recognition of this historical reality has become the legal reality of Canada. This country was settled by European people and the founding relationship was European and Indigenous on a nation-to-nation basis...equal-to-equal. And the terms of the settlement in the European sense were "at our pleasure."

JH: *How did the idea of a stewardship council come about?*

ML: The idea of shared jurisdiction on a sovereign-power to sovereign-power basis has always been the basis for our idea of management of n'Daki-Menan. We've always been willing to share our home—the terms were set out in 1763 [the Royal Proclamation of King George III] and still exist in constitutional law. This is our homeland and other people chose to live here, and shared jurisdiction is a fair and equitable way of allowing for this.

The stewardship council idea came quite a few years ago. We can't agree with the whole notion that aboriginal ownership—our natural ownership of the land—should be something government recognizes only if we will sell it. Selling land removes you from control of your own destiny since everything else that goes on around you is uncertain. We need something better than this. It's discriminatory—why do Indians have to sell their land? Our full participation in Confederation is not particularly repugnant to Canadian society or any theologies in Canadian society. In fact we see it as beneficial.

JH: *What would you say are the bottom line requirements for design of the Temagami Stewardship Council if it is to play a successful role in resolving conflicts in Temagami?*

ML: First, that we have a practical, working role in the shared jurisdiction. In the four townships, implementation of this concept will become a reality and, as the new land-use regime, we must expand this to the balance of n'Daki-Menan to achieve what we require for certainty for the future life on the land.

Second, the principles we take to it are those of sustained life and lifestyles—if the land dies everybody else does too. We are at the highest point in Ontario, at the headwaters for three main river systems. So there is some sanctity in this and this has to be understood and appreciated. We need fresh air, fresh water and food...together with fire, this is what we need to survive.

Then, finally, making decisions regarding human use of the land which would allow for land to dictate the level of development and the kind of development because its integrity needs to be protected. And that is the bottom line.

15

The Need For Local Currencies

Robert Swann

As most of us know only too well, political power cannot be divorced from economic power. So it is no coincidence that, at the same time that our political institutions have become more and more centralized, our money and banking systems have suffered a similar fate. Few people, however, seem to regard changes in such financial systems as one of the possible avenues for significantly increasing the power of local communities. Conventional wisdom sees banks and money as unchanging features of the modern landscape.

Robert Swann has spent much of his life inventing and encouraging the implementation of alternative-model institutions that allow communities more economic self-reliance. Considered the "father" of the community land trust, he is President of the E.F. Schumacher Society in Great Barrington, Massachusetts. At a time when the international monetary system appears that it might have reached a critical size threshold, his argument for restoring local currencies and local banks makes compelling sense.

The opportunity now exists to develop a better money system than the one we use at present. We need a system which will, by its nature, promote and enhance small scale institutions, including small businesses, cooperatives, small communities and local towns. We need a system that will support and encourage the local supply of local business, and that will allow farmers to make a living producing food for local consumption. In short, a regionally-issued currency is essential to creating a diversified, stable, regional economy made up of many interrelating small businesses.

Although I am not a specialist in this area of monetary economics, I have studied money for many years, and it is clear to me that the specialists have been looking too closely at the elephant's trunk and are not aware of its other parts:

1. the fact that regional currencies are rooted in the tradition of American history and were an important factor in the tremendous early growth and development of America;

2. that centralized banking and currency issuance, though part of the national growth of the country, are no longer appropriate to the needs of people and, in fact, have helped lead to ever-increasing concentrations of wealth in urban areas and to poverty in rural areas;

3. that reintroducing regional currencies at this time can help to revitalize agriculture and culture in rural areas or regions which have been left behind in the over-centralization of wealth in the cities; and

4. that there are several critically important changes to be made in the structure and policies of regional banks in order to avoid the mistakes of recent centralized banking as well as the mistakes of local banking in the last century and before.

*

Money is a tool we use to allow goods and services to pass among those in the community and among communities. It is a piece of paper that allows us to get the things we need or need done from the people who produce them without making a direct trade of the thing or things we produce or services we perform.

One important rule about the creation of money is that the amount of money created must equal pretty closely the amount of production at a given time. If there is money out there representing more goods and services than are really being produced, the value of that money goes down. This is inflation, or, more precisely, "devaluation," because the value of the currency is less. Prices inflate because the currency has devalued.

On the other hand, if there isn't *enough* money created, people no longer make exchanges. This is deflation, one of the major symptoms of a depression.

Every region has its own distinct character that makes it different in very critical ways from other bioregions. It has its own resources, both natural and human, particular to the kind of land there and the people who live on it. Therefore each bioregion has its own unique productive capacity. Since the creation of money, in order to avoid inflation or deflation, should increase or decrease with the amount of production at any time, it is essential that the supply is created at the local or regional level by institutions which are focused on their own regions. In fact, the Federal Reserve System was designed on a decentralized basis with 12 districts throughout the country, each bank within the district issuing credit/currency in making commercial loans.

Supposedly, this system would create money as needed within the district, and to some degree it does. But since the ultimate control of the system lies with a national board, decisions of the board are made in the "national" interest. The national interest may be in the interest of some parts of the country, but not in the interest of other parts—generally not in the interest of the rural areas, which have been increasingly deprived of the necessary money to develop a diversified economy. The result is extreme disparity between different regions of the country.

*

Many people assume that our centralized banking system goes back into very early history. In fact, in the U.S. at least, it is a relatively recent development; money institutions were small scale and decentralized through most of history. They consisted of either direct exchange of goods by barter or, later, exchange with metals (gold or silver) of intrinsic value. Banking as a system grew slowly out of the medieval period when goldsmiths became, first, the caretakers of gold and, later, became bankers by using the gold as a reserve for redemption.

The banking system that grew out of the medieval period was, by and large, very diversified, with many banks issuing their own currencies. This condition existed right down to the present century. I have in my possession actual bank notes issued by four different banks in New Hampshire during the last century.

"The town of Woergel in Austria pulled itself out of the depression in a matter of months after the town issued its own scrip, or currency."

But by the end of the last century, or the beginning of the present century, along with the centralization of power in the nation-states which then emerged, banking systems were centralized and came increasingly under the control of the nation-state, as it happened here in the United States. Although the centralization of banking was a growing development by the last half of the 19th century, it was not until 1913 that a central system became formalized with the Federal Reserve Act.

Centralized banking and control of money creation had grown hand in hand with the industrialization of the country in the 19th century. As industrialization grew, the need for larger amounts of money to finance the large industries with their "economies of scale" grew also. Huge sums of money also meant the need for big banks, and big banks need many depositors. The greatest concentration of depositors was in the cities. As the banks and the cities grew, the smaller rural banks were drawn into the agglomerations. Big banks, and their big industrial customers, could pay higher interest rates to depositors. The smaller banks began sending their deposits into the central financial cities. Thus cities and industrialization grew apace, fueled by money ever more centralized in the big banks. This movement really took off with the advent of a national currency, the Federal Reserve Note.

This was helpful to industrialization, employed many people, and also helped to make the nation grow, in a sense. But a major problem has been that the centralization of the system has served to centralize the *benefits* of the system as well.

The effect on the small farmers and rural economies has been devastating. The current "farm crisis" is only the latest dramatic and highly publicized manifestation of what is really a *monetary* crisis that dates from the Federal Reserve Act. Credit for small scale farming and the small rural businesses that support it had so dried up even before the Depression of the 1930s that the U.S. government had to create the Farmer's Home Administration in order to help replace—with tax money—some of the rural credit that had been lost to the large cities.

My point is that a very large part of our lives is controlled or governed by a system over which we have little or no control and do not understand. To a large extent we have accepted unconsciously a system of money and banking and we are asleep in our relationship to it. Perhaps no one fully understands this system—even many of the bankers who use it—but it is an important factor in determining what happens in our lives, for it determines who gets credit to start what kind of business where.

The hopeful side is that there is a strong interest in wanting to become more conscious in all of our relationships. This is the first step which must precede the creation of a new money system to replace the old.

*

The replacement of national currencies with local ones, as I have suggested, is to be only partly new. In the early part of the century, small local banks issued their own currency and were a major reason, according to John Kenneth Galbraith in his book *Money*, for the rapid development of the country. This was the so-called "free banking" era of U.S. history which began to bring about Thomas Jefferson's dream of a nation of small, independent, self-reliant farmers.

During this period, these banks provided money and credit for small farmers to produce and sell their goods. How were these banks different from banks today? Well, for one thing, being in small towns, the bankers knew the people they were dealing with in a personal way. They could make loans on the basis of "character" and not merely on the basis of the collateral which an individual could put up to protect the loan. Today loans are made in a very impersonal way: everything depends on "track record," and if you don't have a "track record," as most young people do not, you can forget it.

Perhaps most importantly, this local currency created by each bank could only circulate in a limited regional area, unlike national currency which easily leaves local banks and is swallowed up in the financial centers to finance giant projects of large corporations. Small businesses did not have to compete for credit with larger businesses in other places, as they do now that deposits are pooled in the urban areas. Credit decisions made locally could be made by people with particular personal knowledge not only of the borrowers, but also of the needs of the region as a whole.

*

During the Depression of the 1930s—a period of deflation world-wide—many new forms of exchange appeared. These serve as examples of the usefulness and efficacy of locally issued currency in the face of the failure of a national currency. One example of such a scrip system was in the town of Woergel in Austria. It drew international attention at the time and was investigated by Yale economist, Irving Fisher. Fisher wrote that the town of Woergel pulled itself out of the depression in a matter of months after the town issued its own scrip, or currency.

I learned of another example, closer to home, in a discussion with the present editor of the *Springfield Union News*. He was just a copy boy during the Depression but he remembers that the publisher at that time, a many by the name of Boles, paid his employees in a form of scrip which Boles printed himself with his name on it. He instructed his employees to use the scrip to purchase goods or services from advertisers in his paper, and he would accept it in payment for advertising. This worked very well apparently, and, in fact, to everyone's surprise, it began circulating around the entire town when people who didn't work for the paper accepted it as change for purchases at the paper's advertisers' businesses. In other words, it didn't require redemption in advertising; people simply accepted it as if it were national currency. "I'll take Boles money, it's just as good as the Federal money!"

One more recent experiment in the local issue of currency took place in 1972 when, at the age of 87, philosopher Ralph Borsodi and I issued a currency in the town of Exeter, New Hampshire. The currency was based on a standard of value using 30 commodities in an index similar to the Dow Jones Average. He called this currency a Constant, because it would remain constant in value over time, unlike the national currency. This currency circulated around the town of Exeter for over a year, proving, as Borsodi had hoped, that people would use currency that was not the familiar greenback. At the time, it received national publicity in *Time* and *Forbes* and other magazines. When asked by a reporter if his currency was legal, Borsodi suggested that the reporter check with the Treasury Department. He did, and the answer came back, "We don't care if he uses pine cones, so long as they can be exchanged for dollars to pay taxes."

Borsodi discontinued his experiment after a year or so, but he had accomplished his purpose—to demonstrate that it *can* be done.

*

One of the major arguments against "free banking" in the 18th century, indeed the one that persists today, is that the many small local banks which issued their own money sometimes failed and this hurt many of their small depositors. Some of these banks truly were run by scoundrels who created money for non-productive purposes such as helping their friends buy land for speculation. The feeling was that such abuses could be controlled if money were issued centrally.

"Local currencies could play a critical role throughout the bulk of America in the development of stable, diversified regional economies now bypassed by our centralized banking system."

But decentralization and diversity have the benefit of preventing large-scale failure. This is as true in banking as it is in the natural world. For example, take seeds. If many different strains of corn are used by different farmers, some seeds will produce more than others; but if a disease hits the crop, some strains will resist and the total effect will not be disastrous. However, if all farmers have shifted to a new hybrid seed and a blight hits this type of seed, the result can be widespread disaster.

This, in fact, has happened. The diversity of banking and money issue in the early 1800s had this advantage. Today, however, we are facing the failure of the entire system.

This is not to say that local or regional currencies will automatically avoid the twin pitfalls of inflation and deflation. The question is, on what basis should money be issued in order to avoid them—particularly inflation?

Money has to be issued somewhere by someone, or some institution. In reality, every one of us involved in trading of any kind creates money whenever we buy something and exchange our IOU for the goods or services bought. In return, we must produce something of value to add to the supply of goods and services. Our IOU will only be as good as the confidence other people have that we can and will produce something of value. In other words, confidence is at the heart of banking. What, then, will provide confidence in regionally-issued currency?

I believe that some form of redemption in a locally produced commodity will be essential—at least in the short term. If confidence is created and maintained over the long term, redemption may be unnecessary. To maintain confidence over the long term, certain elements and policies must be established from the beginning:

1. Whatever organizational form is adopted, it should be a nonprofit structure, in order that it be perceived and understood by the public as an organization which will not line any individual pocket.

2. It should be democratic, with membership open to the residents within the bioregion, who elect members of the board. This is the same kind of structure we have developed for the Community Land Trust.

3. Its policy should be to create new credit for short term, *productive* purposes only. Productive, short-term credit means credit for up to three months for goods or services already produced and on their way to market, or credit which finances the interim period between production and sales. Clearly this is not inflationary. Other issues of typically productive short-term credit are for crop production, such as seeds and fertilizers and tools which pay for themselves in a very short time. In this respect, warehouse receipts may be used in exchange for local currency. Mortgages for housing, industrial construction, etc., are not legimate for issuing money, but must come out of savings.

4. Such regional banks must also be clear of any governmental control other than, perhaps, inspection, in order that investment decisions are not based on political motivations.

5. Finally, the newest element which must be introduced into banking is the use of both social and ecological criteria in making loans to complement the financial criteria. We already have the beginning of this element in the general field of "social investment," and more specifically in the development of Community Investment Funds. Social investment

criteria for making investments in the conventional investment field use what are called "social screens." Total investment in this field has now reached the billions of dollars, and is growing rapidly. Community Investment Funds, while still in a much more modest stage of development, use a more positive set of social criteria than those in the conventional field and are limited to specific geographical areas. Funds such as these could combine with hard-pressed local banks to initiate regional currencies.

*

Issued according to these guidelines, local currencies could play a critical role throughout the bulk of America in the development of stable, diversified regional economies now bypassed by our centralized banking system. In fact, if I am right about runaway inflation coming in the future—or, as some economists are predicting, a serious depression—such currencies will again become necessities, perhaps sooner than we would think.

16

A Metamorphosis For Cities: From Gray To Green

Peter Berg

With the vast proportion of the world's people predicted to be living in cities by the turn of the century, the sustainability of these metropoles has become a matter of extreme urgency. Pollution, transportation, energy, housing, the provision of water and food, and the impact of the city on the surrounding region are among the key questions facing city planners. At the heart of all of them, however, is the question of power. Devolving the modern "city-states" into self-governing and participatory neighborhoods actively aiming for self-reliance and overall regional sustainability is perhaps the key challenge of the age.

Peter Berg and the Planet Drum Foundation took up this challenge several years ago with the adoption of a wide-ranging "Green City Program" for San Francisco and other Bay area towns. Fundamental to this initiative is the integration of ecological and political concerns.

Cities have changed in fundamental ways since the middle of this century. They have become incomprehensible and dangerous, and their future is one of the most important planetary considerations confronting humankind.

The largest are two and three times the size New York was in 1950 when, with eight million inhabitants, it was already considered to be impossibly huge. At present Mexico City leads with over 22 million. Tokyo and Sao Paolo, among others, have only a few million less. Whatever their current size, nearly all cities will continue to grow at a faster rate. About 100 metropolitan areas with at least five million people are projected for 2025, three times as many as there are today.

Cities this big can't be known intimately. The historically relatable cities such as ancient Athens, Pepys' London or even Walt Whitman's Brooklyn have disappeared, replaced by enormous puzzles that look extremely different from each person's position in them. Consider that many cities are more populous than entire small nations, some containing as much as half of their own national populations. No longer merely the centers of countries, they have become independent organisms whose constantly changing sets of systems continually move beyond knowledge and control.

Cities also demand too much from their bases of support, overreaching local bioregions to pull resources from thousands of miles away. For example, Los Angeles drains water from northern California, extracts coal for electrical power from the Great Basin's Four Corners area, and ships in liquefied natural gas from Indonesia. As cities continue to expand, there is ever-increasing competition for the same water, energy and food resources. These are running out faster than planners could have imagined before the population boom of the last few decades. Even now, administrators don't realize how vulnerable to chaotic shortages and supply breakdowns cities have become.

Once a rare and privileged way of life supported by a large agriculturally-productive rural population, city-dwelling is fast becoming the norm. In spite of the fact that they are grotesquely overgrown compared with the recent past, over-extended and subject to crippling disruptions, urban environments will soon be the primary inhabitation sites for our species. As late as 1950, less than 30 percent of the world's population lived in cities and towns of 25,000 or more. But by the year 2000, half of humanity will no longer live on the land. In some places the figure will be much higher: over 75 percent in Latin and North America, Europe, East Asia and Oceania. Fewer people are remaining in direct contact with nature at a time when more urbanites need to somehow produce part of the resources they consume.

Cities not only restrict beneficial contacts with nature, they inexorably surround and destroy it. Open spaces that previously separated urban areas fill in with new development to encircle natural areas like cages in a zoo. A nearly unbroken megalopolis runs down North America's eastern seaboard from Boston to Atlanta that is, in effect, a wall barricading wildlife from the ocean. Cities bordering on rivers sprawl further and further along the banks to thinly stretch and finally break the all-important water links of ecosystem chains.

Metropolitan areas have the densest population, so they are the places where most resources are consumed and most wastes are produced. Consumption levels for industrialized countries are excessively high in general and sometimes outrageously bloated. Outright squandering of resources is commonplace and can be plainly seen in hydrant water pouring down gutters for hours, newspapers and packaging littering streets, and hundreds of thousands of unneeded electrical lights burning all night.

The effects of city-generated wastes and sewage are often less visible but much more perilous. Rivers, lakes and bays near urban areas are universally subject to some degree of pollution, sometimes so high that they become devoid of aquatic life. Soil and underground water near garbage landfills are contaminated with deadly concoctions. Air-borne factory smoke and traffic exhaust kill nearby forests and poison far-distant lakes. When controls are attempted, they can be quickly out-dated by the sheer volume of urban growth—reducing harmful emissions from each automobile by half still means more smog if the number of cars triples—and fresh disasters are constantly being discovered.

"The first step toward reconceptualizing urban areas is to recognize that they are all situated in local bioregions within which they can be made self-reliant and sustainable."

These are large-scale problems whose simultaneous effects are capable of cracking the foundations of our present social and political concerns. Many cities have begun to reveal a neglected and grim side that forecasts a meaner future. Their wounds show openly in ruined inner districts, abandoned and burned-out buildings, rows of broken windows in empty factories, debris-filled vacant lots and pot-holed streets. Further growth will lead to deepening crises such as can now be found in Mexico City: declining job opportunities as more people arrive, housing shortages, growing disparity and animosity between well-off and poorer individuals and districts, withdrawal of whole sections of the city from administrative control and essential services, mounting physical and mental health problems, and decay of basic infrastructures ranging from public education to sewage systems.

Transforming Our Conception Of Cities

A profound transformation is needed in the way cities are conceived. This can't be merely an administrative reform or a change in the design of systems or structures because it needs to involve a completely new set of priorities and principles. The future purpose and function of cities and the activities of city-dwelling must become the focus of social and political consciousness on a primary level.

The first step toward reconceptualizing urban areas is to recognize that they are all situated in local bioregions within which they can be made self-reliant and sustainable. The unique soils, watersheds, native plants and animals, climate, seasonal variations and other natural characteristics that are present in the geographical life-place where a city is located, constitute the basic context for securing essential resources of food, water, energy and materials. For this to happen in a sustainable way, cities must identify with and put themselves in balanced reciprocity with natural systems. Not only do they have to find nearby sources to satisfy basic human needs, but also to adapt those needs to local conditions. They must maintain the natural features that still remain, and restore as many of those that have been disrupted as possible. For example, restoring polluted bays, lakes or rivers so that they will once more be healthy habitats for aquatic life can also help make urban areas more self-reliant in producing food.

Different geographical areas have different conditions depending on their natural characteristics. Bioregionally-founded values that are appropriate to each place should be agreed upon and then used to direct municipal policies. Guides for doing this can be transferred over from some basic principles that govern all ecosystems:

- *Interdependence:*

Heighten awareness of interchanges between production and consumption of resources so that supply, re-use, recycling and restoration become more closely linked. Reduce inequitable exploitation.

- *Diversity:*

Support a wide range of means to satisfy basic human needs and a multiplicity of cultural, social and political expressions. Resist single-interest solutions and monoculture.

- *Self-regulation:*

Encourage decentralized activities carried out by groups in neighborhoods and districts. Replace top-down bureaucratic agencies with grassroots assemblies.

- *Long-term stability:*

Aim policies to work under various conditions and for several generations. Minimize short-term programs and patchwork remedies.

When interdependence, diversity, self-regulation and long-term stability are consulted, it is possible to make much more ecologically coherent and therefore more practical decisions than are generally seen today. Applied to the cycle of food production and consumption, for example, these values could lead to beneficial features: more small-scale farms and gardens near or in the city that employ greater numbers of people, preserve and restore green spaces, reduce transportation costs and provide fresher produce; wider use of permaculture (permanent agriculture) and native food plants to conserve and build topsoil, lower water use and maintain natural habitats; subscription buying by institutions and groups of individuals who spend a certain yearly amount to receive a specified quantity of produce—thereby stabilizing farm incomes and levels of food production; collection of tree and yard trimmings, food scraps and other organic wastes to create compost fertilizer; re-use of urban grey water on farms and in gardens to reduce fresh water consumption; and some type of food production on everyone's part ranging from backyard, rooftop, window box and community gardens to work-sharing on farms.

Each urban area needs to develop an ecologically-oriented Green City Program that delivers a high quality of life for all of its residents in harmony with its bioregion. City greening includes urban planting but extends to much more than re-vegetation. It also means conversion to renewable energy, development of suitable transportation, extensive recycling and re-use, greater empowerment of neighborhoods, support for socially responsible small businesses and cooperatives, restoration of wild habitat, wide participation in planning for sustainability, and creation of new civic art and celebrations.

There are already many separate groups working in various sectors of urban sustainability who can supply pieces of an overall program. They should help in drafting sections of it to authenticate a grassroots approach, introduce disparate elements in the same field, and eventually join together differing concerns under an overarching "green umbrella" to accomplish the massive governmental changes that are necessary. In planning the transition from fossil fuels which pollute and dangerous nuclear power, to renewable sources such as solar, hydro and wind, for example, representatives can be drawn from businesses that manufacture, distribute and install renewable energy equipment, labor groups who will benefit from jobs in those areas and agencies that regulate energy production and use, as well as from alternative energy advocacy and environmental groups.

Here are some examples of changes in municipal policies that might be recommended in different parts of a Green City Program whose implementation would have powerfully transformative effects.

- *Retro-fit public buildings for renewable energy.*

Equip city office buildings, schools, libraries, fire and police stations, and all other structures with some means to produce their own energy from renewable sources.

- *Develop suitable transportation.*

A wide front of new approaches including: company buses and vans to transport workers directly to job sites, point-to-point conveyances to replace use of automobiles for shopping and appointments, in-neighborhood transit such as ride switchboards for local businesses and offices, discouragement of single-passenger automobile use by prohibiting it at peak times and downtown, increased gasoline taxes that are earmarked for light rail construction, and establishment of multiple-use zoning to allow more businesses and institutions to operate closer to where people live and thereby reduce the need to travel to work.

- *Initiate full-scale recycling and re-use.*

Curbside pickup of household organic and manufactured recyclables. Stringent reprocessing of all wastes from industrial processes. Establishment of small-scale neighborhood secondary- materials industries. Require municipal government to purchase recycled materials whenever possible, preferably from local sources. Create grey water treatment facilities so that water now wasted can be used to water lawns and trees, wash vehicles, clean buildings, flush toilets and for other uses that don't require fresh water. Install household units to recycle used wash water for similar purposes.

- *Empower neighborhoods.*

Devolve a large percentage of tax revenues to neighborhood councils and assemblies for direct local use. Provide space and materials to greatly enhance neighborhood communications ranging from meeting places to bulletin boards and even FM radio and cable TV facilities.

- *Assist socially responsible businesses and cooperatives.*

Greater employment and higher levels of prosperity are possible through assisting the creation of sustainability-oriented small businesses and co-ops by providing "incubators" where offices, equipment and materials can be shared. City government should also establish priorities for procuring supplies from these new companies.

- *Restore wild habitat.*

Establish new corridors of native vegetation in the city, linking habitats so that wildlife can move unimpeded through urban areas. To make these corridors, restore creeks where possible by bringing them up from storm sewers.

- *Open the process of planning for sustainability.*

Solicit neighborhoods' visions of their futures and use these as standards for determining changes. Adopt "statutes of responsibility" that charge officials to maintain the health of cities and their inhabitants. Citizens could take legal action against officials if air, water and soil aren't kept free of poisons.

- *Celebrate life-place vitality.*

Assist the creation of small-scale localized media (murals, billboards, markers) that feature natural characteristics. Stage public celebrations of natural events such as seasons and animal migrations. Provide guides to natural sites.

Some of these measures reduce costs and eliminate waste on a vast scale. Most are directly related to greatly improving the health of local bioregions. All of them involve new job opportunities and contribute to self-reliance. And they are only a few examples of the many changes that should be made.

A Future Of "Urban Pioneers"

For a Green City Program to succeed, there also needs to be a radical new consciousness about living in cities on the part of individuals. City-dwelling has traditionally been easier and more luxurious than country life. Residents have been accustomed to services and amenities that were relatively inexpensive and whose continuous supply was not their responsibility. People still assume that water, food and energy will continue to flow into cities as effortlessly as in the past, even though they know that the places where those resources originate have been severely degraded.

"...city-dwellers have to become "urban pioneers" in a concrete, steel and glass wilderness, developing new urban forms and remaking their own lives as they simultaneously recreate the urban landscape."

But the realities of urban life are changing rapidly and will change more drastically in the near future. Since mid-century, utilities, health services, food prices, and housing costs have increased many times over. They will rise even more sharply as cities continue to expand and compete for resources that are diminishing in quantity and quality. Presently, travellers return to comparatively prosperous countries like the United States shocked by the desperate conditions in places like Calcutta, Rio de Janiero and Nairobi. They believe that their own communities are immune to the spectrum of problems that they find there, problems which range from inflation and endless delays to widespread disease and abject poverty. Soon it will become clear that although these calamities have struck Third World countries first, parallel developments are due for many other urban areas. There simply aren't enough basic resources even in developed countries to sustain the huge urban populations that are accumulating.

City life was once mediated and stabilized by social and cultural groupings that occupied particular districts. Established historic and ethnic communities often played the largest part in fostering an individual sense of identity and a personal angle of perception for relating to the city as a whole. These zones of security and belonging have been seriously eroded or completely destroyed and replaced by growing wastelands of anonymity and fear. Their loss is a main reason why cities are now less convivial and more threatening.

Although cities as we know them are on the verge of collapse, people aren't aware of the great changes that are coming. Media coverage is restricted to isolated situations like the plummeting decline of Detroit or abysmal lack of public services in East St. Louis, and politicians are reluctant to air the bad news even as they quietly move to the suburbs. In fact, the city is at a point of major transition. We are beginning to see an historical shift comparable to the birth of the modern industrial city in the late 18th century. Urban people will be obliged to undergo a thorough transformation. To reclaim a positive outcome from deteriorating situations, city-dwellers have to become "urban pioneers" in a concrete, steel and glass wilderness, developing new urban forms and remaking their own lives as they simultaneously recreate the urban landscape. To do this they need to learn new skills, redirect their energy and inventiveness, and align their efforts with the more self-reliant and sustainable vision offered in a Green City Program.

The profile of an urban pioneering life includes these elements: working several part-time jobs rather than a single-employment, 40-hour week; growing some food on a continuous-basis; recycling household wastes and water; re-fitting dwellings for energy conservation and maintaining some means for producing energy from renewable sources; restoring wildlife habitats; reducing or eliminating the use of a personal automobile; developing new cultural expressions that reflect bioregional and planetary themes; and participating in a neighborhood council to decide everything from planning and justice to social services and celebrations. It will replace the often deadening and escape-seeking urban existence of the present with stimulating, highly varied and creative pursuits that are more related to artists and nature-seekers than to factory and office workers. Even in a densely populated metropolis, these new urbanites will be able to claim personal home-neighborhood-villages and be fully involved with them. Many people are already doing some of the things that lead to this transformed urban life. When most people are doing all of them, urban-dwelling will be much richer and more livable.

In a municipality dedicated to carrying out a Green City Program the citizenry could have much greater interaction with government than at present. To accomplish recycling goals, for example, people wouldn't merely put out materials to be collected. They would expect the city to help create jobs by assisting groups and businesses who remanufacture products from those materials, and to purchase them whenever possible, preferably from neighborhood-based companies and cooperatives. The government would be viewed as an instrument for carrying out the residents' intention to make the city self-reliant and sustainable.

Reversing The Present Trends

The future prospect for cities is at a critical juncture. If allowed to continue in their present course, the detrimental affects on people, bioregions and the planetary biosphere will soon reach an intolerable point. Currently 850 million urban people worldwide are squatters: 50% of Third World city-dwellers have no plumbing or electricity. By the year 2000, the number of squatters will more than double to over two billion with a similar acute increase in those living without rudimentary necessities. A nightmarish scenario with billions crowded into urban heaps and living in despairing poverty has already begun. It will surely proceed to even worse stages of routine breakdowns in production and distribution of essential human requirements, collapse of basic infrastructures, extreme conflict between social and economic groups, and governmental chaos.

There is a saving alternative to this painful outcome, but it requires a thorough transformation in the purpose of cities and the ways that people live in them. Bioregionally-oriented governments and ecologically-conscious residents carrying out Green City Programs can end and even reverse the present ruinous trends. Rather than destroying the bases for obtaining resources, we can develop renewable energy, recycle materials and water, and produce food within cities themselves. Rather than destroy natural areas, we can maintain and restore habitat for native plants and animals and increase the number of green spaces. Rather than watch urban areas become more anonymous as they become larger, with more violence, fewer jobs and increasing homelessness, we can empower neighborhoods to carry out community services on a local, personalized and mutual basis.

Cities must change soon and in profound ways, and this huge metamorphosis can be the occasion for a positive shift in consciousness that harmonizes the needs of society with those of the natural systems that ultimately support it.

Workers, Communities And Toxics

Eric Mann

Recently in Los Angeles, the Labor/Community Strategy Center organized a meeting called "Workers, Communities and Toxics: A Two-Day Conversation" in which fifty-five activists from the Latino, Black, labor, and environmental movements came together to explore both the possibilities for multiracial coalitions and potential difficulties in developing such alliances. East Los Angeles residents illustrated their dilemma with the example of the furniture industry, which has proven itself toxic to both workers and the community and yet provides relatively well-paying jobs for tens of thousands of workers. One participant asked how furniture companies could be subject to environmental restraints which would also restrict them from fleeing to nearby Mexico to continue their polluting while even further exploiting their workforce.

We discussed a possible long-term campaign for the furniture industry that would combine changes in the production processes to dramatically reduce poisonous varnishes and coatings. Such a proposal would require low-interest government loans to allow relatively small firms to retool their facilities. Other aspects of this plan included protection for the rights of undocumented workers (the vast majority of the work force); noninterference by the company in union elections; and a long-term commitment by the retrofitted firms to stay in the communities. While this outline is just one of several possibilities and remains in the earliest conceptual stages, it reflects a strategic perspective in which environmentalism is not just a battle against chemicals, but a kind of politics that demands popular control of corporate decision-making on behalf of workers and communities.

Fundamentally, the environmental crisis is a crisis of institutional and corporate production. Acid rain, global warming, pollutants in the air, pesticides, and internal combustion engines are products of the chemical, atomic, automobile, electrical, and petroluem *industries*. But any efforts to limit or shape production in environmentally sound ways will involve direct confrontations between the "management right" to determine what a corporation will produce and the rights of workers and communities to work and live in safety. Strategies to build effective and democratic trade unions that could break with the current union pattern of slavish obedience to corporate priorities in return for short-term economic benefits for workers, as well as strategies to build city-wide and regional coalitions across the boundaries of color, gender, and race, become central to the creation of an effective environmental strategy that might hold corporate executives and elected officials accountable for the ecological impact of their policies. We will need new models for political and economic life—models that combine representative government "at the top" with significant power for direct input into decisions at the grass-roots level, from both workplaces and communities impacted by any given decision.

"...environmentalism is not just a battle against chemicals, but a kind of politics that demands popular control of corporate decision-making on behalf of workers and communities."

Yet this kind of democratic impact will be resisted by corporations, and will only be achieved if we have a transformation of labor unions as well as the development of powerful community coalitions. Oppositional movements in the labor movement, like Teamsters for a Democratic Union or the United Agricultural Workers New Directions, need to integrate the legitimate demands for union democracy and better contracts with a more fundamental challenge to the toxic processes and products that characterize contemporary production in many firms. Ultimately, workers must demand a comprehensive program for a nontoxic economy, and support worker retraining and income maintenance in the process of moving our economy in an ecologically sound direction. Community coalitions must be formed which attempt to develop regional economic plans from the bottom up, and which can work together with the unions in a larger struggle for ecological sanity. This focus on transforming the corporations may seem rather utopian, but it is far more realistic than the present electoral and lobbying strategy that imagines that toxins can be effectively regulated within our present institutional matrix.

The deepening ecological crisis requires that we move to strategies that can actually address the full depth of the crisis. This necessarily will involve a more rational planning of production and uses of resources. Yet only a powerful grass-roots movement could plausibly develop the strength to counter those corporate interests which will continue to oppose rational planning.

As progressives once again debate the merits of a radically reformed capitalism versus new models of democratic socialism, it is important that the content of "economic democracy" center on the replacement of our present model (in which private corporate power dominates public life) with new models of public power and decision-making rooted in workplaces and communities.

Radical social problems demand radical political solutions.

17

Two Kinds Of Power: A Different Experience At Oka

Helen Forsey

The power of people in place endures beyond military might and even superficial "defeat"—a fact well-known by this continent's native peoples. Canada's Mohawk crisis of 1990 demonstrated not only the resilience of native cultures—once again tested to the limit and beyond—but was also a profound learning experience for those non-Native people involved in a supportive Peace Camp established close to the trouble-spot.

Helen Forsey, a peace activist and founder of Dandelion Community in Ontario, was there at the Peace Camp. Here she describes some of the experiences—both hard and inspiring—that many of us might have to go through if we are truly to put power back in its place.

The summer of 1990 saw a long-simmering crisis explode between Mohawk and non-Native authorities at Oka and Kahnawake, near Montreal in Québec. At Oka, the Mohawk community of Kanesatake had been peacefully blockading a proposed golf course expansion into their ancestral pine forest for four months, when the swat team of the notorious Sûreté du Québec (or SQ, part of Québec's provincial police) moved in to enforce a court injunction against them. The SQ's vicious attack on the blockade was repulsed by armed Mohawk "Warriors" and one policeman was killed. That same day, in solidarity, Mohawks at Kahnawake, 30 miles away, blockaded a main bridge linking up the highway through their reserve with Montreal—an action which infuriated thousands of non-Native commuters. There followed a bitter, 11-week standoff.

When the Canadian Army moved in on Oka at the end of August, some 50 Native men, women and children held out against it in the Kanesatake Treatment Center. Under conditions of extreme hardship and aggressive provocation, the "People in the Pines" remained non-violent, while the governments, the army and the police became ever more repressive, effectively suspending basic human rights.

In September of 1990, at the height of the "Oka Crisis," a group of over 100 people, mostly Natives, camped in a park on the outskirts of Oka to demonstrate solidarity for the People in the Pines. Like the standoff we were there to witness, the Peace Camp was a confrontation between different kinds of power: on the one side, the power of people who have endured through thousands of years in this land, whose cultures affirm the connectedness of all life; on the other, that of a racist, patriarchal order which has brought life to the brink of the abyss.

The experience of the Peace Camp was a microcosm of the larger struggle, illustrating many of the same issues and dilemmas faced not only by Native people, but by all those who choose life-affirming values in the face of violence, injustice and despair, and who seek to empower themselves accordingly. I was privileged to be part of the Oka Peace Camp for its final ten days. What follows are glimpses of that experience, and of the learnings I continue to draw from it.

*

Midnight. We know we have arrived when we see the Sûreteé du Québec searchlights turned on a motley collection of tents and vehicles in a field to the right of the highway just before a police roadblock. At the Camp gate, we are greeted by a security patrol and directed to a school bus, where an outrigging of tarpaulins and shelving glows yellow in the light of a lantern and campfires. We talk a while. Finally, exhausted, we sleep.

Morning. A sunrise ceremony around the Oneida fire. Tobacco is burned and prayers said for the People in the Pines. Now breakfast is cooking, delicious smells wafting out from the tarped-in kitchen area by the bus. Kids run around, laughing. People are gathering again—a greeting circle for the group that came in last night, a van-load of people from the Seminole Nation of the Florida Everglades. Each of them speaks to the circle in their language, and one translates into English. They speak of how they heard of what was happening here at Oka, of how they managed to come, of what is in their hearts for their sisters and brothers here so far to the North.

A stroll down to the gate acquaints us with the rest of the Camp layout:

dozens of tents and a teepee, a number of fire circles, two other kitchens, the porta-potties that a local supporter has arranged for. The "gate," where the Park road turns off the infamous Route 44, is flanked by signs and banners: "Solidarity with the Native People," "Peace and Justice," "We Love the Mohawks," "Pas d'Armée—Négotiez!" and "If You Like South Africa, You'll Love It Here." The eerily symbolic name of the hill behind the Camp is incribed on an official Parks Department sign: "Calvaire d'Oka"—Calvary, the hill where, long ago, another man who stood for peace and justice was crucified.

Facing the highway is a row of flags, most of them unfamiliar to us, for they are the flags of First Nations that we non-Natives scarcely knew existed. Beneath them the sacred fire is kept perpetually burning, with sweetgrass, tobacco and cedar in containers nearby for ceremonies. "Elijah's Fire," they call it. It was lit by Elijah Harper, the courageous Cree chief from Northern Manitoba who, as a member of that province's Legislative Assembly, blocked the passage of the infamous Meech Lake Constitutional Accord just two months ago. The Accord would have enshrined a racist version of history in our very constitution, and would have made redress of the multiple injustices done to aboriginal peoples even more difficult. Elijah Harper, with his eagle feather and his clear, quiet "No," has became a heroic symbol of native resistance.

"I've felt so privileged, so laden with gifts, in the middle of a bloody war zone!"

We heard about the Camp by word of mouth; there is next to nothing about it in the news. For one thing, there has been no effort made in that direction; people are not here to play to the media; they are here to demonstrate the power of nonviolence, and to use it to gather peaceful energy and send it over the hill to the People in the Pines. By and large, what is happening here does not even look like "news." Indian people cooking, playing with their children, tending ceremonial fires, gathering to share information and prayers while helicopters circle overhead and the police and Army roll past on the road—these are hardly the images the authorities want to promote as they step up their aggression against Native people. Besides, by this time, after almost two months, Oka itself is "old news"—as are the grievances of First Nations peoples right across this land.

As the days go by, we find our ways of fitting in. This is not the kind of organization we are used to, where things are usually made explicit;

instead, we find ourselves honing our observation skills and our sensitivities. We learn to pay attention to many things, keeping our eyes and ears open, figuring out how we can be useful. There is always plenty of work to do: cooking, getting firewood or water, picking up garbage, doing dishes, building shelters with tarpaulins or plastic to withstand the September gales, taking our turn on security. People are constantly dealing with the multitude of messages, needs and decisions that arise, and hoping always for news of some progress towards a peaceful resolution of the conflict that has brought us all together here. There is laughter, and teasing, arguments and hugs, excitement and quiet times.

Relatively quiet, that is. For always in the background is the noise of the traffic on Highway 44, much of it made up of SQ vehicles, Army trucks, jeeps and armoured troop carriers taking youngsters in uniform to what we pray will not be a combat experience. We greet them as they pass; sometimes there is no response, sometimes they shout insults or make rude gestures. The SQ has taken over the park facilities opposite us; at times there are as many as 20 SQ cruisers massed near the roadblock 50 yards from the Camp gate. They observe us constantly through binoculars; occasionally they taunt us, drumming mockingly on the hood of a car or making their version of war-whoops. Every little while an Army helicopter flies over, buzzing the Camp to disrupt our gatherings and show us the 50mm machine guns bristling from the front.

We watch their shows of military might, pondering the fear and weakness they betray. We wave to them sometimes, or take pictures, as they do of us. At night their high-intensity searchlights illumine our sleep, and our dreams are troubled.

Nor is this merely token harassment. In fact, we at the Camp are getting a taste of the psychological warfare that the Army and the SQ have been using to try to break the spirit of the People in the Pines. The third afternoon we are there, the SQ sets up yet another roadblock on Highway 44 at the Oka Monastery, to prevent anyone without SQ accreditation from entering the "perimeter"—now arbitrarily expanded to include the Camp. This means that we are forced to engage in constant negotiations to get them to allow food or medicines in; new arrivals are turned back under threat of arrest. It is demoralizing to know that our friends and supporters are out there, unable to get in; newcomers are being told that there is no longer any Camp. Anyone who leaves, even to buy groceries or get gas, is barred from re-entering. They have jammed our cellular phones, and even urgent messages are able to get in and out only through the help of a couple of supportive Oka residents. As time goes on, the harassment escalates, rumors are rampant, and a certain siege mentality grows. Only the patience, steadfastness, and irrepressible humor of these people keeps us going, as well as the realization that, given how hard the authorities are trying to get rid of us, it must be important for us to stay!

The irony of it is that we are a Peace Camp. Surrounded by military hardware, suspicion and hostility, the Camp is an incredible statement of peace and loving solidarity. It is a spontaneous coming together of people from all over Turtle Island, from the Four Directions: two Inuit sisters from Hudson's Bay, Micmacs and Malaseets from the Maritimes, Okanagans from British Columbia, Métis from Saskatchewan and Maine, Seminoles from Florida, Cherokees from Oklahoma and Tennessee, Crees, Sioux, Ojibways and other Algonquins, Oneidas, Cayugas and Mohawks, as well as non-aboriginal people from both nearby and far away. Many of us have temporarily abandoned families, businesses, classes or jobs in order to be here.

"You fill up and you spill over, and that's the power of it. Sharing that power increases it. It's the very opposite of our culture, where power is something you hoard."

During most of the Camp, 90 percent of the people here have been First Nations people, and much of the conversation and most of the prayers have been in Native languages. For those of us who are non-Native, being in the minority has been instructive in many ways. For one thing, we have had an incredibly rich opportunity to learn from and about Native people—to glimpse their cultures, their traditions, and their lives and struggles under the domination of our society. Many of us came here with our own understanding and experience of the power of nonviolence, and the Native elders and their people have added new dimensions to that understanding.

One non-Native woman from the Camp described it this way: "I think of the vast beauty of all the people I've met: a whole community, women and children and men, all ages. All the stories I've heard, of these people's lives and what they've gone through: I've felt so privileged, so laden with gifts, in the middle of a bloody war zone! To be guests of these people—to be offered their stories, their rituals, their circles—so many impressions, like fingers touching my heart and leaving their mark. Their gentleness, the eloquence with which they spoke and moved, their accessibility—we were hanging out with national leaders! Their humor: I'd be there fuming, enraged at what was happening, and they'd come with this extended hand and this fabulous joke! I saw the true sophistication, the agelessness, the maturity of their culture, and how much we need that. These are people who have been thrown against the wall, decimated by our society. It's so foreign to our culture to be so positive in the face of such ugliness."

This is not to suggest for a moment that there were no internal problems or contradictions in the Camp; there were. With so many people of different traditions gathered together under such challenging conditions, it would have been ridiculous to expect otherwise. Conflicts, resentments and mistrust arose from many sources: personality clashes, leadership styles, disputes over the appropriateness of male/female "roles," the participation of non-Natives, the specifics of the best ways to support the People in the Pines or to respond to the constant threats of eviction or arrest.

The power of the experience resided in how these differences were dealt with. When divisions arose, a circle would be called, attended by everyone. Holding the eagle feather in turn, each person would speak their thoughts and feelings: anger, frustration, confusion. *All* were listened to with respect; then support was offered. "We have resources here for this," they said, "spiritual people, medicine people. Use them. We have to be of one mind. Not only for ourselves and for our people, but for the police, the government as well." As people shared that message, the tension began to dissolve. It was the beginning of a healing process with a broader base, far beyond that circle itself.

We heard afterwards how this same process had been happening inside the Treatment Center. The power generated in the Camp was somehow linked to theirs, each supporting the other. And we all knew that was why we were there.

Key to the transformations that happened at Oka was the phenomenal strength of Native people simply living and affirming their traditions. Another non-Native participant in the Camp spoke later of "watching the inventors of democracy practise it. Listening and speaking: it was so simple, it was stunning. You fill up and you spill over, and that's the power of it. Sharing that power increases it. It's the very opposite of our culture, where power is something you hoard."

*

Although the experience itself was far more than any analysis of it can convey, it is still possible to identify some of the elements of the power that we shared, Natives and non-Natives together, camped there in the field below the hill at Oka.

Part of it was certainly the simple stubbornness of Native resistance:

the sense, the knowing, that all this has been going on for generations, and will continue, no matter what the immediate outcome of this particular set of events. When the Park authorities, and then the SQ, would tell us we had to leave, the circle would discuss it and decide to stay. At one point a proposal to move the whole Camp elsewhere was put forward to the group as if it was a decision, but the Clan Mothers pointed out that the process had not been followed: they had not agreed. The men's directive was never retracted, but the women simply ignored it and went on about their business. The few people who had started to take down their tents soon realized that they were the only ones doing so—and the tents went up again. Another strong element was the power of nonviolent action, familiar already to many of us: the power of "clinging to the truth," of doing what you know to be right without counting on any particular outcome of your action. This disconcerted the authorities and the media alike, who were used to dealing with strategies and tactics, with publicity stunts and symbolic actions done for public effect, but not with this dogged determination, this commitment to some invisible and far-from-assured purpose.

Another part of the power was the strength of the alliances we formed, and especially the spiritual forces that drew us together across racial, cultural and gender lines. The importance of "being of one mind," born of our political understanding and reinforced by the ceremonies and circles that formed the spiritual core of the camp, gave us a strength of which the SQ and the Army had no comprehension, and against which they were powerless.

Vital to our power was our groundedness, our direct connection to the Earth, living there together beneath that wooded hill under the September sky. Our daily activities—gathering wood, cooking, caring for the children, building shelters, cleaning up, keeping warm, and sharing everything we needed in order to do so—drew us together as a community and bonded us to that piece of ground. It is no accident that much of the work that forged these bonds was "women's work". In cultures the world over, women traditionally are responsible for the tasks most directly concerned with maintaining and nurturing life and people's connectedness with each other and with past and future generations. Such work is concrete and essential; it is the stuff of life. Moreover, such work constitutes a major part of the basic survival activity of any community, Native or non-Native, which does not depend on "modern conveniences." Living this reality together redeemed us from much alienation. We were rediscovering the things that really matter, in a context where we could interpret those discoveries and integrate them into the totality of our spiritual and political lives.

Later on, of course, the SQ and the Army won their victory. They harassed and deceived us into dispersing, then finally evicted the remainder of the Camp and arrested the half-dozen who flatly refused to leave. Although some of us later regrouped at Kahnawake, the elements that had made the Camp at Oka so powerful were changed or gone. The group that stayed on for a while at the Kahnawake bingo Hall was mainly men, and mostly non-Native; the daily tasks of living in the open were replaced by the perversions of watching violent television or microwaving junk food in an over-heated, over-lighted, echoing concrete structure designed and built for profiteering—a monument to the alienation that our society has tried to force upon people everywhere. No wonder the spiritual center was gone; no wonder the divisions and resentments grew; no wonder the commitment to nonviolence withered in such a place.

"Vital to our power was our groundedness, our direct connection to the Earth, living there together beneath that wooded hill under the September sky."

And yet, the government, the police, the Army, the death culture have *not* won. The discouraging events of late September were not the end, although they culminated in the capture and imprisonment of the People of the Pines as they left the Treatment Center. As the Native people have known all along, the struggle continues. In Oka, in Kahnawake, in communities across this land, and in our hearts, the power we experienced at the Peace Camp continues to grow and flourish. To quote again one of the women of the Camp, "I believe that more people than ever before know now that none of us will survive without the Native people of this land. More people know now what real power is and where that power is coming from—the kind of power embodied by women, by children, by Native cultures. All lifeforms on this planet are telling us that we must embrace that power. I know that spirit, that power, will survive, not because of what we wish, but because of what we *know*—because of our human history."

Epilogue

Since September 1990, the objective situation of the Mohawks and other First Nations peoples living under the thumb of Canadian governments has, if anything, deteriorated. Money—and therefore legal help—is in short supply for those arrested at Oka and Kahnawake, and many of them face long terms as political prisoners. Police harassment continues in their communities. Kanesatake Mohawks have found new survey stakes in the Pines, and even the land that was promised to them has yet to be handed over. The Federal government is said to have funded an anti-traditionalist faction to engage in negotiations on behalf of the community. The Parliamentary Committee looking into the crisis is a sham. Across the country, court decisions, government policies and budgets continue to deny Native peoples' basic rights, and to expose the brutal racism of Canada's internal colonial system.

Yet Native people continue their centuries-old traditions of resistance, bearing witness to a power and a wisdom older than oppression itself, and fired by a new determination born in the "Indian Summer" of 1990. It is their spirit which must inspire us all—Native and non-Native—to continue the struggle for the kind of power that will render all oppression obsolete.